A PEOPLE OF HOPE

Ian Cowley

Highland Books
Guildford, Surrey

Copyright © 1993 Ian Cowley

British Library Cataloguing-in-Publication Data. A catalogue record for this book is available from the British Library

Published by Highland Books, an imprint of Inter Publishing Service (IPS) Ltd, 59 Woodbridge Road, Guildford, Surrey GU1 4RF.

All rights reserved. No part of this publication may be reproduced or transmitted in any form or by any means, electronic or mechanical, including photocopying, recording or any information storage and retrieval system, without either prior permission in writing from the publisher or a licence permitting restricted copying.

In the United Kingdom such licences are issued by the Copyright Licensing Agency, 33–35 Alfred Place, London WC1E 7DP.

All Scripture quotations, unless otherwise noted, are taken from the *Holy Bible, Revised Standard Version*.

Typeset by Electronic Book Factory, Fife.
Printed in the UK by HarperCollins Manufacturing, Glasgow.

ISBN No: 0 946616 91 4

CONTENTS

	Page
Acknowledgements	vii
Maps	ix
Foreword	xi

PART ONE: PREPARE THE WAY OF THE LORD

CHAPTER
1	Prepare the Way of the Lord	3
2	The Tornado	9
3	The Three-Fold Journey	15
4	My Journey	26
5	Sweetwaters	39
6	Learning to Serve the Poor	46
7	The Floods	61

PART TWO: A PEOPLE OF HOPE

8	The Violence and Suffering	71
9	The Response of White Christians	84
10	Standing for the Truth	97
11	The Local Church in Action	113
12	Learning Obedience	134
13	The Importance of the Local Church	153
14	The Challenge of the Poor	174
15	The Inward Journey	187
16	The Way Forward – Our God Reigns	197

Notes 209

ACKNOWLEDGEMENTS

This book began its life in 1988, when I was invited to preach at the Good Friday three-hour service at St. Agnes Church in Kloof. Because of the events taking place around us at that time, I decided that instead of using the normal pattern for the three-hour service, I would speak about the local church as a community of the cross. It has taken five years for the book to be completed. I owe an enormous amount to many people, without whose help, encouragement and support this book could never have been written. Above all I am very conscious of the guidance and grace of God who has sustained and directed me throughout this project. To God be the glory, great things He has done.

I particularly want to thank Derryn Hurry who spent many hours helping me with details of the manuscript, and whose encouragement and belief in the value of this book has meant so much to me. I am also very grateful to Sally Wynn who typed the manuscript, and retyped it, and retyped it again! Others who have helped me greatly with their ideas, advice and support include Michael Cassidy, Calvin Cook, Edward England, Andrew Judge, James Moulder and Gerald West. I would like to thank David and Pene Brady in Hilton and Mike and Rosemary Murphy in Sheffield, who gave me a place in which to write when I needed somewhere quiet, away from the demands and pressures of my work.

The support of Alison, my wife, and John and Grace, my children, has been unstinting, in spite of the sacrifices which 'the book' has often demanded, and I am deeply grateful to them.

Lastly I want to express my gratitude to the people of the Church of the Ascension, Hilton. It is a privilege to belong to such a Christian community. My prayer for this book is that it will be an encouragement to our church, and to many other churches, as well as a testimony to what God has done, and a help to others who are wrestling with similar issues.

Ian Cowley
Hilton

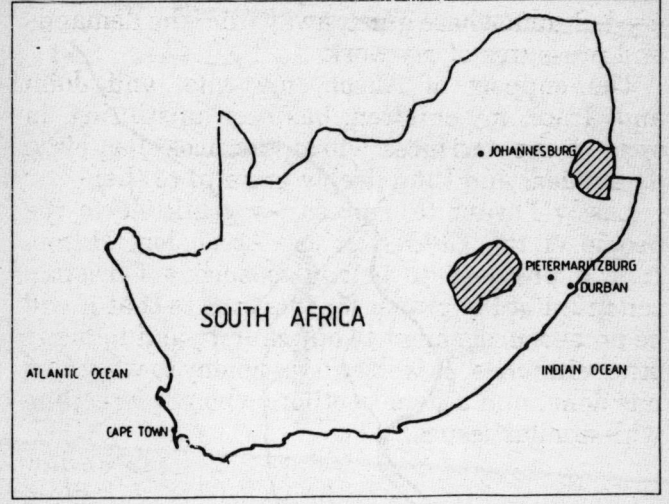

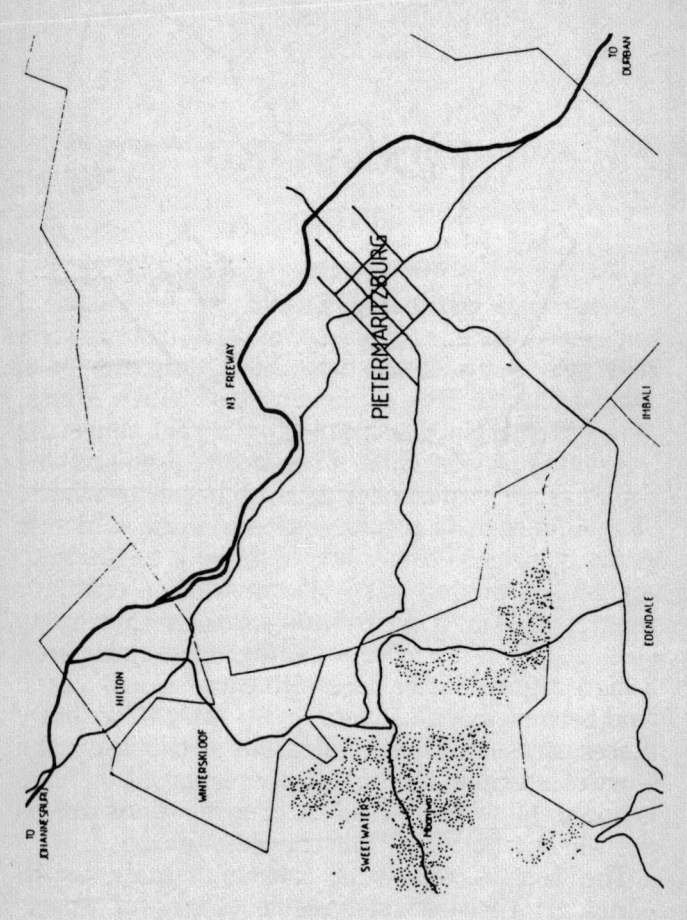

FOREWORD

Ian Cowley is my pastor. The Church of the Ascension is my home church. So I suppose I am biased. Even so, I am ready to affirm my view that this is one of the most intriguing stories of a local church ever to come out of South Africa. And because South Africa is in a real sense the laboratory or workshop of the world, it means this book has relevance for local churches everywhere. Not because it is a huge success story, which it does not profess to be, but because it is the honest soul-searching story of one rather ordinary congregation's struggle, along with its pastor, to be a people of hope in a context of despair, and a sign of good news in a situation of bad news. And because hopelessness is the story in so many places across our tired old planet at this time, the story of a people who have become a people of hope is one to be widely noted by congregations across the world who covet that characteristic.

The book's context of course, namely South Africa in the last convulsive stages of apartheid madness, is not only captivating but massively challenging. How does an ordinary congregation of ordinary people, mainly white in this instance, cope with a context of massive racial oppression, prejudice, injustice, inequality, poverty and endemic violence, along with a few natural disasters like floods and tornadoes thrown in to boot?

It's quite a story actually, again I say not because it's all success, but because it is reflective in integrity of genuine odyssey, pilgrimage, pain and finally a real sense of progress. Here is not a pastor and people saying 'We've arrived.' Far from it. But they are saying 'Wherever you are in your congregation and local church, won't you be part of the processes of pilgrimage, pain and progress with us because we have found this fits both our Lord's precept and practice, and beyond that it brings forth a precious and powerful sense of His presence?'

One of the special features of this book is the way it reveals how Ian Cowley, who is a big person in spirit and largeness of heart, has laboured hard to see not just his own gifts but the gifts of each person in the congregation released into service. The book has practical hints for the perceptive pastor on how to go about this and so will be specially helpful and challenging for ministers. But likewise for lay people who in many places despise, minimise or suppress their gifts and so end up never having the joyous fulfilment and growth opportunities which come from being 'equipped for the work of the ministry' (Eph. 4:12). For the lay person to miss their ministry destiny and place in any local church is not only a personal and a congregational tragedy, but a community and social tragedy too. For the needs out there in the society and community are massive, and lay person, dear lay person, they won't be met without you.

Foreword

You, yes you, need to be released into service and Cowley's book will point the way for you. So why don't you let him jolt you from a seat in the grandstand to a place on the playing field. You might also find it a heck of a lot of fun!

One must also register that the book has a very particular and pervasive challenge relating to the ministry to the poor – especially from people of privilege who generally think little of the poor. Nor has it just been ambulance ministries to victims of poverty or oppression but a prophetic ministry challenging and calling for structural change where unjust structures constitute a major part of the reason for the poverty.

It is important and instructive also to note here that it was through the spirituality and renewal which entered the Church of the Ascension through our previous rector, and was built on by Ian, that this powerful motivation developed among numbers of our people to take this rare ministry of concern for the poor not only into their hearts but into some profound and ongoing practical action. Beyond that, while not all the congregation became involved in the practical side, most have taken this concern into their consciousness, their praying and their giving.

In my own view none of this would have happened apart from that base of spirituality and renewal which I would see as a prerequisite for any local church wanting to move out in this way. In other words, it is the work of the Holy Spirit to produce witnesses (cf. Acts 1:8). Cranking up a programme with some Better Business Bureau techniques and publicity will never do it. But have Holy Spirit renewal, along with sustained biblical teaching on discipleship and its implications, in other words, get the foundation and the first things first, and all else will flow as fruit from root. In Cowley's terms, it is the upward and inward journeys which produce the outward one. I'd say that was as close to a spiritual law of Medes and Persians as I could think of.

So here is a fine book about a pastor and people caught up in a serious struggle to unite both song and service, both prayer and precept, both proclamation and practice, both word and work, both pain and progress, and all in a context of true worship where liturgically there is a heartwarming and relatively rare blend of form and freedom.

As I said, it's quite a story and one which I think every pastor and lay person, not only in South Africa, but wherever the Lord's people gather, should read.

You won't regret it.

Michael Cassidy
Pietermaritzburg, June 1993

Part One

PREPARE THE WAY OF THE LORD

CHAPTER 1

PREPARE THE WAY OF THE LORD

> The beginning of the gospel of Jesus Christ, the Son of God. As it is written in Isaiah the prophet,
> 'Behold, I send my messenger before thy face,
> who shall prepare thy way;
> the voice of one crying in the wilderness:
> Prepare the way of the Lord,
> make his paths straight –'
>
> (Mark 1:1–2)

So begins the Gospel according to St. Mark. Mark is quoting from the prophet Isaiah, who foretold the coming of a messenger, sent by God, who would prepare the way for the glory of God to be revealed to all people. John the Baptist's role was to call the people to repent, to turn back to God. He came to prepare people's hearts for a great and utterly unique event – the coming of Jesus Christ into the world.

Many people today have a strong desire to know God, and to be close to God, and to do his will. But we find this very difficult. All kinds of things get in our way, and we ourselves seem to be a large part of the problem. How can we prepare the way of the Lord in our day, in our lives, and in our world? How do we go about finding God, knowing him and doing his will, in a world which is changing so rapidly and which is so full of problems and suffering?

This book is an account of the experiences of one local church in South Africa, as we tried to take seriously these very searching questions, and to be obedient to God in some difficult and challenging circumstances. In this book I am writing about my experience over nine years as the Rector of the Church of the Ascension, an Anglican parish church in the town of Hilton, in South Africa.

Hilton is a small town close to the city of Pietermaritzburg, the capital of the province of Natal. Until the repeal of the Group Areas Act in 1991, Hilton was a 'white' area, although there are many black people who live here, mainly as domestic workers or gardeners. Only a few miles away, however, is the black area of Sweetwaters, in which thousands of Zulu people live, many in great poverty and need. The population of Hilton is around 4,000 while the population of Sweetwaters is probably in excess of 100,000 people. We estimate that of the total population of Sweetwaters, only about 40 per cent are actually employable. The rest are widows, cripples, old people and children. Of those who are employable, less than half actually have any sort of job. Whenever I travel from Hilton to Sweetwaters, I feel that I am leaving one world and entering another. It is like moving from one country to another, but of course this is simply the reality of life in South Africa. The results of apartheid are all

Prepare the Way of the Lord

around us. The suffering caused by apartheid has overwhelmingly been borne by blacks. But apartheid has also brought its own oppression to the white people. It is impossible to live at peace with oneself when one is aware, even to a small extent, that one is constantly enjoying privileges that are denied to other members of the community largely because of the colour of their skin. Apartheid has in one sense given whites an easy life, but in another sense it has made life very difficult and painful and challenging. As a result many whites have chosen to leave South Africa and to build a new life in another land, away from the challenges and the dangers of the land of apartheid. Thanks be to God, the system of apartheid is at last being dismantled. But the problems caused by apartheid will be with us for many years to come. The reality of life in South Africa is division and separation, with enormous disparities in wealth, opportunity and access to social services such as education and health care.

This in particular poses enormous challenges for anyone who is seeking to be obedient to God and especially to be a true disciple of Jesus Christ. How do I live in the comfort and luxury of white South Africa and still maintain my integrity as a disciple of Jesus Christ? How much of my affluence am I able to keep, and how much should I give away? In what ways should I get involved in changing the system of white privilege and black deprivation and oppression, which confronts me wherever I go?

I personally have tried to take seriously these questions and challenges. So also has our local church, and while there are many areas where we fall far short of the standards expected of disciples of Jesus Christ, we have also learned much, as we have sought to work out what it means for us to be obedient to Jesus, in our society and our circumstances.

This book is divided into two parts. The first part is the story of the journey that our local church has taken together over these past nine years. The second part concerns the principles and lessons that we have learnt during this journey. I have tried to extract some principles for the life and ministry of the local church, and these are expressed in particular in Chapter 13.

Our awareness of their significance developed through the experiences recounted in the first section of the book. The narrative and autobiographical sections thus, I believe, are important in enabling the reader to understand how and why we are able to speak in these terms about the importance of the local church. The interviews with members of the congregation in Chapters 11 and 12 also will help the reader to hear, through their own voices, the stories of individual people of the local church.

This book is also partly about the problem of being an affluent white Christian in an unjust society. White South Africans are the beneficiaries of an extremely unjust system and we have all, Christian and non-Christian alike, had the benefit of this. But then many of us who are in this position have also heard and wrestled with the call of Christian discipleship. We have had to ask, what are the options for Christians in this society. Firstly, we could walk away from it, and leave. Secondly, we could attempt the way of total renunciation of our privilege and place in society. Then there is a third way of living inside the tension and the ambiguity. This book is, in a sense, a report of where we have got to, in wrestling with these options. We haven't found the final answer. But we have decided that we are going to try to do the kind of thing that the Bible and the tradition of the church suggest that Christians ought to do in these kinds of situation. We are trying to take Scripture and the church seriously, and to work out what this means for us, in the place in which we find ourselves.

The fact is that nobody in the church can say, 'Here is a ten-point programme to deal with this situation. Go and do this and you'll be okay'. We have to 'work out [our] own salvation with fear and trembling'. (Phil. 2:12) We have to discover for ourselves what obedience to Christ means in our own particular situation in Hilton and Sweetwaters. But we can say, 'Here are the resources of the Bible and the church, and the answer is to be found by drawing as fully as possible on these resources.' The key is to take these resources and translate them into actions, and so to live out our faith, as many people in our church have sought to do.

So this book is not an attempt to create a theology of the church nor is it an attempt to expound the biblical teaching about the rich and the poor. This is a story about what we as a congregation at the Church of the Ascension have learnt about living with the tension of the affluence and poverty of our society, which may be of some use to other Christians, who are grappling with similar questions. I have tried to set out what we have made of the concept of living as a people of the church and a people of the Scriptures, in South African society. Our conclusion is that there *IS* a third way, a way of hope in Christ for those who are called to be a people of hope, because of the hope he has given us.

CHAPTER 2
THE TORNADO

'What do you think we should be looking for, Dave?' I asked. I was driving along a dusty Natal road in the parish car, a Ford Cortina station wagon. Next to me was Dave A'Bear, a member of the parish who was working among the Zulu people of Sweetwaters. In the back of the Cortina were sixty loaves of bread, which we had hastily bought. We were heading for a rural community in the Impendhle area of the Natal Midlands, far away from the main towns and roads. The reason for our journey was that a devastating tornado had struck this area the previous afternoon, Thursday, 24th November, 1983. I had arrived at the Church of the Ascension at the beginning of September, 1983, and I was still trying to find my feet in the new work. Gradually I was getting to know people, building relationships, and determining my priorities. I was wanting to learn and to be open. But I also had some fairly clear ideas about the church, about what its leadership should be doing, and about the need to get involved where people were suffering.

I had read about the tornado in our local paper, *The Natal Witness* at breakfast that morning. During our morning prayers at the church, I felt a conviction that we should go and be with the people who had suffered and whose homes had been destroyed. Immediately after our prayers I said to Dave, 'I think we should go out to Impendhle. What do you think?'

'Yes, I had the same thought,' he said. 'When shall we go?' 'I think we should go now. What are you doing this morning?'

Neither of us were doing anything which could not be put aside and a short while later we were on our way. We did not know exactly where to find the village which had been hit; but we knew that it was close to a particular road, and that if we travelled along that road, we would in due course find the scene of the disaster.

It took us about an hour to get there. First we saw the crumpled wreck of a car which had been physically lifted off the road by the force of the wind, and hurled a couple of hundred yards across the side of the hill. Fortunately the woman who had been driving the car had stopped and run away before the full force of the tornado had hit it. Now it was nothing but an almost unrecognizable twisted piece of metal. Trees were broken in half, branches scattered far and wide. As we drove over the top of the hill we saw the village. There was a strange quietness about it, although there were four or five vehicles parked by the side of the road, and little pockets of activity here and there.

We parked the car and walked across the veld to the village. Roofs had been ripped off houses, corrugated iron torn in half and thrown all over the place. The evidence of the sheer power of the wind was staggering. Fortunately most people had been able to find shelter, hiding under tables or curling

The Tornado

up on the floor. Nevertheless two people had been killed, and a number injured, and many houses had been badly damaged. We were particularly struck by the sense of shock, of numbness, that was apparent in the people. It was as if they simply could not take in what had happened to them, here in this remote little community on the side of a hill, under the African sky. They could not understand, could not even react to this incredible force which had suddenly come upon them from nowhere and devastated their homes and lives in a matter of seconds. We spent about two hours there wandering around, giving a loaf of bread to anyone who wanted one, saying simply: 'The Lord be with you', or 'God bless you', in our broken Zulu. There did not seem to be much need for long conversations; we just wanted them to know that someone cared. Eventually we walked back to the car and headed for home.

As we drove home I pondered over what we had seen and done. If such a disaster had hit a small white town it would have brought forth a massive response. A disaster fund would have been set up and people would have been taken away to places where they could sleep and recover, while they tried to sort out their shattered homes and lives. Very little of this had happened for this community. There were front page stories in the newspapers, and even the main item on the television news that evening concerned the Impendhle tornado. But after that it was largely forgotten. The area was too far away, and the people's names would mean nothing to those who read the newspapers and watch T.V. There would not be much real public concern or interest in the need and loss of a small community of Zulu people somewhere in the Impendhle district. So, I asked myself, what was the point of our going out there? Were we just a couple of do-gooders, perhaps trying to ease our own sense of guilt? What had we actually achieved?

As I thought about these things, I felt clearly that it had been right that we had gone. We were able to drop everything and go, in a way that many people could not have done. And the point of it was not to do something for the people. It was simply to be with them, in their time of grief and loss. It was to be able perhaps to show them that we cared; that for us, the love of Christ meant that we wanted to try in some way to comfort them and to be near them. When I arrived home at about 1 o'clock that afternoon I knew that I would not quickly forget what I had seen that day.

This was my first experience since arriving in Hilton of a major human tragedy. South Africa has increasingly become a land of tragedy. Terrible human tragedies, which would cause enormous shock in any civilized land, are happening all the time. They appear in the newspapers and then disappear, many of them to be forgotten and never to be heard of again. But for those who have suffered, these awful things will never be forgotten. South Africa is a land of suffering and pain and yet it is also a land of great riches and beauty. What, I had to ask myself, is the Christian response to living in circumstances like these?

When I arrived in Hilton in September, 1983 as the new Rector of the Church of the Ascension, I came to an Anglican parish church which had the reputation of being strong and alive. This

The Tornado

congregation had been greatly influenced by the charismatic renewal which had affected many churches in South Africa in the 1970s. The Church of the Ascension was however a church with a long history. It was founded in 1904, and the present church building was dedicated on Ascension Day, 9th May, 1907. For many years the church had been very much a traditional Anglican parish in its character and worship. The charismatic renewal had brought many changes. There was a considerable increase in numbers, and a strong emphasis on commitment, obedience to Christ and the empowering of the Holy Spirit. The main Sunday worship became known for its exuberant praise and powerful preaching and teaching. However, there had also been problems of which I was very aware when I arrived in Hilton. The previous Rector had left the Anglican Church in a controversy over the issue of baptism, amongst other things, and a number of the leading members of the church had gone with him. So I knew that my new job was going to be challenging in more ways than one.

Simply being both a white South African and a Christian involves enormous challenges and dilemmas. I have already mentioned some of the questions that were very important to me at that time. I was still in my early thirties and this was my first appointment as Rector of a church. I wanted very much to be a leader who would enable the people of our church increasingly to be an authentically Christian community. But where should I begin? How does a church in a prosperous white South African community become the kind of Christian community that Jesus would want us to be?

These were the questions that I was wrestling with when I arrived in Hilton to take up my new appointment. I was determined not to allow these issues to slip gradually into the background under the pressure of the daily demands of parish work. Yet I knew that there were few, if any, simple answers. I had, as the leader of a local church, to be true to the gospel of Jesus Christ and, at the same time, not escape the implications of the gospel for South African society. I knew that what was needed was not talk or good ideas. What was needed was action. I had to put into practice what I believed about the church. But how was this going to work out?

CHAPTER 3
THE THREE-FOLD JOURNEY

The Christian life has often been described as a journey. One song puts it like this:

> We are pilgrims on a journey
> We are brothers on the road
> We are here to help each other
> Walk the mile and share the load.[1]

The Christian pilgrimage has many times of joy and laughter, but it also involves much bearing of burdens. It is a journey that we undertake with Christ, and so, if we are to continue faithfully to walk with him, we are going to find ourselves sharing both his peace and his pain. The two go together, and often we experience them both at the same time, with one being the main theme, and the other more quietly there in the background, but nonetheless present and real.

This journey of faith can also be seen as a three-fold journey. It is a journey towards God, but at the same time it is a journey towards one's self and a journey towards those around us. There is the upward journey, the inward journey, and the outward journey. All three are essential components of a genuine seeking to know God.

As we come to know God for who he truly is, we find that we ourselves are profoundly challenged and changed. We also find that we are drawn to the needs of those around us, because God is love, and his love is always reaching out in tenderness and compassion to those who are in need. This is clearly expressed by Jesus in Matthew 22:36–40. Jesus was asked by a lawyer, 'Teacher, which is the great commandment in the law?'

> And he said to him, 'You shall love the Lord your God with all your heart, and with all your soul, and with all your mind. This is the great and first commandment. And a second is like it, You shall love your neighbour as yourself. On these two commandments depend all the law and the prophets.'

The whole teaching of the Bible is summed up in loving God and in loving our neighbours as we love ourselves. The three-fold journey can be seen also in the first chapter of Mark's Gospel, in the passage which immediately follows the description of John the Baptist. In Mark 1:9–15 we read:

> In those days Jesus came from Nazareth of Galilee and was baptized by John in the Jordan. And when he came up out of the water, immediately he saw the heavens opened and the Spirit descending upon him like a dove; and a voice came from heaven, 'Thou art my beloved Son; with thee I am well pleased.' The Spirit immediately drove

him out into the wilderness. And he was in
the wilderness forty days, tempted by Satan;
and he was with the wild beasts; and the
angels ministered to him. Now after John was
arrested, Jesus came into Galilee, preaching
the gospel of God, and saying, 'The time is
fulfilled, and the kingdom of God is at hand;
repent, and believe in the gospel.'

Here are three distinct phases in the life of Jesus,
which correspond to a three-fold journey.

The upward journey

Jesus came to the river Jordan to be baptized by
John. As he came out of the water the Holy Spirit
descended upon him like a dove, and he heard the
voice of the Father saying, 'Thou art my beloved
Son; with thee I am well pleased.' This marked
the beginning of the public ministry of Jesus. He
received a very clear word of affirmation from the
Father, which must have been very significant
to him. Throughout the Gospel accounts we find
many references to the very close relationship
between Jesus and the Father. Jesus often rose
very early in the morning to go off into a quiet
place to pray, and to spend time renewing his
relationship with the Father. In this way he
was able to cope with the enormous demands
made upon him by the crowds, as well as all
the other conflicts, frustrations and difficulties
which came both from his enemies and from his
own disciples.

The falling of the Holy Spirit upon Jesus at his

baptism is also very significant. In Jesus Christ we see the perfect example of a man who is filled with the Holy Spirit. He declared in the synagogue in Nazareth, 'The Spirit of the Lord is upon me.' (Luke 4:18) After his resurrection Jesus told his disciples, 'Behold, I send the promise of my Father upon you; but stay in the city, until you are clothed with power from on high.' (Luke 24:49) All followers of Jesus need to be clothed with the 'power from on high', the power of the indwelling Holy Spirit, the Lord, the giver of life.

So Jesus began his public ministry with an act of obedience to the Father, namely, his baptism by John. He submitted to this, not because he needed to be cleansed of sin, but because he knew that his whole life was to be a yielding to the will of the Father and, at the same time, a complete identification with the human race, in all its weakness and need (see Matt. 3:13–15).

Jesus is the Son of God, the second person of the Holy Trinity, God the Son, God in human form. He is truly God but he was also truly and fully human. It is important for us to remember this as we seek to follow him, because it reminds us that he was a real human being just like us, and so he is able to show what we are meant to become. He came to serve the suffering and the sick, the outcast and the sinners of his society. He knows our needs and difficulties, and understands them because he experienced them himself. So he is able to show us the way forward, as he calls us to follow him, to be different, to become more and more like him.

The upward journey is our journey to the Father, in and through his Son, Jesus Christ. We begin this journey by responding to the words of Jesus in Mark 1:15: 'Repent and believe the good news!' (NIV). As we turn away from our old sinful self and believe in the Lord Jesus Christ, we also begin to experience the presence of the Holy Spirit within us. Jesus said 'When the Counsellor comes, whom I shall send to you from the Father, even the Spirit of truth, who proceeds from the Father, he will bear witness to me.' (John 15:26) So it is the Holy Spirit who bears witness to Jesus, who makes Jesus real to us as our living Lord and Saviour. And it is Jesus who is the way to the Father. So our upward journey is a journey to God, God in all his fullness, Father, Son and Holy Spirit.

The marvel of the Christian faith is that in believing and following Jesus Christ, God becomes real to us in a way which is both very personal and life-transforming. We find that we can say, with Christians of every age, that God is our God, that we know in our deepest being that he loves us, and in response to this extraordinary experience, which we know to be true and real, we can also say that we love him. We are able to cry from our heart of hearts, as did the psalmist so many years ago:

> I love thee, O Lord, my strength.
>> The Lord is my rock, and my fortress, and my deliverer,
>> my God, my rock, in whom I take refuge,
>> my shield, and the horn of my salvation, my stronghold.
> I call upon the Lord, who is worthy to be praised,
>> and I am saved from my enemies.
>
> (Psalm 18: 1–3)

This is what Christian spirituality is all about. It is to know God truly and to know his unfailing love. And the witness of Christian believers over the past twenty centuries is that this indeed is possible for each and every one of us. Through the life, death and resurrection of Jesus we can know God and be reconciled to him. Paul says 'God was in Christ, reconciling the world unto himself.' (2 Cor. 5:19 KJV) The Holy Spirit makes these things real to us, and enables us to share the love of God with those around us.

This is the key to all that the church is seeking to do in South Africa. The church has a major role to play in bringing about change. But what is the church's primary task? It is not just a matter of changing structures and bringing water, roads and schooling to those who are impoverished. These things must happen, but much more is involved in shaping the future of this land. Unless we recognise this we are in danger of trying to change social structures without satisfying the hunger of human hearts. The greatest hunger in this land is the hunger for love, for the love of God, and for love of our fellow human beings. The answer for the church and for the world surely lies in what St. Paul says in Romans 5:5: 'This hope does not disappoint us, for God has poured out his love into our hearts by means of the Holy Spirit, who is God's gift to us.' (GNB)

The inward journey

Mark tells us that after his baptism in the Jordan, Jesus was immediately led by the Holy Spirit into

The Three-Fold Journey

the wilderness, 'And he was in the wilderness forty days, tempted by Satan; and he was with the wild beasts; and the angels ministered to him.' (Mark 1:13)

This was a time of being alone for Jesus, and it was a time of testing. It was a wilderness experience in more ways than one. Many people find peace and strength through going away and spending time in a lonely place, in the mountains, or at a deserted beach. But for Jesus this was more than just a retreat from the world for a while. It was a time when his inmost motives and thoughts about himself were put to the test, sifted and clarified. Matthew's Gospel tells us that he was tempted in three particular areas. First he was tempted to turn stones to bread. In other words this was the temptation to put his physical needs and desires before his calling to be obedient to the Father. Secondly he was tempted to leap down from the pinnacle of the temple in Jerusalem. The devil said to him, 'If you are the Son of God, throw yourself down; for it is written, "He will give his angels charge of you," and "On their hands they will bear you up, lest you strike your foot against a stone."' (Matt. 4:6) Jesus replied, 'Again it is written, "You shall not tempt the Lord your God"'. I understand this to mean that we are not to expect God to serve us. God is not someone who is always available to us to do whatever we want, whether it be to satisfy our whims or doubts or our physical needs and desires. Because he is God, we are rather to serve him, and to obey his commandments and his precepts.

Then thirdly, Jesus was tempted to seek worldly power and glory. For Jesus this would have meant abandoning his calling from the Father, and giving himself instead to the will of Satan. 'Again, the devil took him to a very high mountain, and showed him all the kingdoms of the world and the glory of them; and he said to him, "All these I will give you, if you will fall down and worship me."' (Matt. 4:8, 9) And again Jesus resisted the temptation, declaring, 'Begone, Satan! for it is written, "You shall worship the Lord your God and him only shall you serve."' (Matt. 4:10)

Jesus was being tempted to accumulate power to himself, instead of obediently following the Father's will for his life. His response to his third temptation reveals a principle which must govern all Christian attitudes to worldly power and reputation. We are to worship God, and to serve only him. If we allow anything to come before God in our lives or in the church this will severely wound our ability to be faithful in serving him. To worship other gods, of any description, is idolatry and is therefore a fatal compromise in true devotion and obedience to God.

When we think about these three temptations, we come to recognize that deep attitudes are involved here, attitudes which to a greater or lesser extent affect every human being. Jesus had to face the demands of his hunger, and the common temptation to yield to the mastery of our physical appetites. He wrestled with the power of self, which even seeks to make God its servant. He knew the allure of wealth and worldly power and was able to place this in subjection to the will of God for his life. These attitudes are not changed or purified easily. A journey inward, led by the Holy Spirit, is necessary. This is the path to spiritual growth. In my time at the Church of the Ascension I have found that this is an essential part of the Christian journey for us today just as it was for Jesus at the beginning of his ministry.

The outward journey

In Mark 1:15 we find a summary of the message that Jesus preached. One could say that this is the gospel in a nutshell.

'Jesus came into Galilee, preaching the gospel of God, and saying, "The time is fulfilled, and the kingdom of God is at hand; repent, and believe in the gospel."' (Mark 1:15) Jesus is saying that the expectation of the Old Testament for the coming of the Messiah is now fulfilled. The kingdom of God, God's rule or reign here on earth, has broken through into human history in the person of Jesus Christ. And so a response is demanded. 'Repent, and believe in the gospel.' There are many ways in which one could answer the question, 'What is a Christian?' But above all a Christian is someone who repents and believes in the gospel of Jesus Christ. This, says Jesus is how we enter the kingdom of God.

Jesus' ministry on earth, prior to his arrest and trial, was largely concerned with doing certain things in order that people should repent and believe in him. He preached, he taught, he healed the sick, he cast out demons, he showed compassion on needy and suffering people in many different ways. He spoke over and over again about the kingdom of God and about our need to turn away from a self-seeking approach to life, and to receive by faith the good news of God's kingdom. He also trained his disciples to do the same things that he was doing. In Luke 9:1–2 we read how he called the Twelve together and sent them out to preach the kingdom of God, to cast out demons and to heal the sick. In Luke 10:1, 'After this the Lord appointed seventy others, and sent them on ahead of him, two by two, into every town and place where he himself was about to come.'

This is the outward journey, the active involvement with the needs of those around us. Jesus was concerned with every dimension of human need, but most of all he was concerned with spiritual need. 'How blest are those who know their need of God; the kingdom of Heaven is theirs', he said. (Matt. 5:3 NEB) He sought to turn people away from seeing things purely in terms of the material and the visible world. He said, 'You cannot serve God and mammon.' He criticized religious leaders who tried to improve their reputations by an outward show of how religious and devout they were. He called people to turn back to God, in penitence and faith and to seek first the kingdom of God and his righteousness.

So also for disciples of Jesus today there is this outward journey. It will involve bringing the good news of the kingdom of God to those who are spiritually lost. It will also involve asking, 'Who is my neighbour?' and acting upon the answer to that question, in order that we may love our neighbour as ourselves.

This three-fold journey has become real to us here at Hilton particularly through involvement in the neighbouring black area of Sweetwaters. We have been involved in the proclamation of the

The Three-Fold Journey

gospel to those who are spiritually hungry and thirsty. At the same time we have been concerned with many aspects of addressing people's physical and material needs – feeding hungry children, bringing water and sanitation, providing flood relief, building houses for widows, taking the sick to hospital, and so on. These are aspects of the outward journey in our Christian pilgrimage. At the same time we have been very conscious of both an upward journey through the worship and the empowering of God which we have experienced, and an inward journey of self-discovery led by the Holy Spirit, which has brought about deep changes in our perceptions and motivations. Following Jesus has proved, for us, to be a three-fold journey. There may seem to be three journeys, but they are really one.

CHAPTER 4
MY JOURNEY

My journey, my pilgrimage, has been a journey towards God, but it has also been a journey set in the context of a particular society, namely South Africa. I find that I cannot separate one from the other. I am a particular person, the person he made me to be, and I am seeking to find God, to know him and to serve him in particular ways and circumstances. So it is for all of us.

However, the issues which we face in South Africa are not only relevant to this one situation. They are issues which face probably the whole of human society, and which are likely to become more and more urgent as we get closer and closer to the twenty-first century. They are the issues of the longing of the human heart for meaning and purpose, the cry of the poor, the homeless and the weak, and the need for reconciliation across the barriers of race, culture and language. Those who are materially rich are so often spiritually empty, while the poor of the world have so much to offer to those who will only open their eyes and their hearts. If the Christian faith can help to provide healing and solutions in the huge problems of South Africa then surely this will be something from which the rest of the world can come and

My Journey

learn, and find hope for the healing, not just of one nation, but of this whole planet.

I am a South African. I was born in Witbank, Transvaal, and I grew up first in a number of mining towns in Natal and the Transvaal, and then on a farm in Northern Natal. From an early age I went to boarding school, and I attended two well-known Pietermaritzburg schools, Merchiston and Maritzburg College. My family's roots go back to the early days of colonial Natal. My great-great-grandfather, Isaac Cowley, came out from England with his family to Natal in 1859. He became well-known as a builder of chimneys in the early sugar mills up and down the Natal coast. He was also an energetic and dedicated Baptist lay preacher, and he played a leading part in establishing the Baptist Church in early Natal. A stone laid by my great-great-grandmother at the building of the first Baptist church in Pietermaritzburg can still be seen today in Chapel Street, at the site of the present Central Baptist Church.

So for me both the Christian faith and the nation of South Africa are deeply part of my identity, and indeed my very life-blood. They are part of who and what I am, and they always will be. Yet how in this time of crisis in South Africa, can I put the two together?

I grew up in a Christian home and I have always believed in God and in Jesus Christ. However, it was not until I was a university student, at the age of twenty-one, that I began to take seriously the call to follow and obey Jesus Christ as Lord. This happened for me when I went one summer to a Student's Christian Association work camp at a remote mission station at Kentani in the Transkei.

I was deeply struck by the devotion and love for Jesus which I saw in the missionary who ran this mission station. He was a man named Harry Oosthuizen, whose life had a powerful impact upon many students besides myself. For the first time that I can remember, I encountered someone whose life seemed to me utterly and completely dedicated to the love and service of Jesus Christ. This showed itself in everything about him: his character, his faith, his simplicity of life, his love for everyone who came across his path. After less than a week at the Kentani Mission (the Xhosa Evangeli Bible School) I knew that Jesus was incontrovertibly the Way, the Truth and the Life. I knew this not because of what I had been told, but because of what I had experienced and seen with my own eyes. I could not escape from what I knew with my heart of hearts to be the truth, the fulfilment of so much that I had been brought up to believe in and to know to be right. So I sat down in a mealie (maize) field one Friday morning in December 1972 and very deliberately counted the cost and surrendered my life and my will to following and serving the Lord Jesus Christ. After that my life has never been the same.

My Christian upbringing had been largely within the Anglican Church in South Africa. The kind of Christianity which I discovered at the Kentani Mission was very different. However, I was not inclined to reject my Anglican background. Rather I saw what I had now myself experienced as the fulfilment of what I had intellectually believed and accepted for a long time. The challenge now was to live it out. I had seen in Harry Oosthuizen that following Jesus above all meant laying down your

My Journey

life, and bringing his love to whomever he may call you to serve. It meant becoming the servant of all, because of the overwhelming reality of the love of Jesus which filled those who surrendered their lives to him. This was the way in which I had now determined to live.

I first started to work out the implications of this new direction in my life on the campus of the University of Natal in Pietermaritzburg. I became involved in the organizing of a major mission to the University in 1973, in partnership with Michael Cassidy and African Enterprise. Michael Cassidy had, in 1962, launched African Enterprise as an evangelistic organisation which aims to win the cities of Africa for Christ. In 1973, A.E., as it has become known, organised a major conference in Durban called the South African Congress on Mission and Evangelism. This was held in conjunction with two large Billy Graham rallies, in Durban and Johannesburg. I enrolled to be trained as a counsellor for the Durban rally, and began to absorb something of the vision and emphases of these ministries.

By 1974 I was chairman of the local Anglican Society which was a thriving Christian fellowship on the campus at that time. More and more my thoughts were turning to my own future. I knew that I did not want a career in business or law, which had been my plan when I left school. My thoughts had turned to teaching or to a career in broadcasting. The new South African television service was about to begin at that time. I went for an interview with SABC personnel officers to talk about a possible career as a television producer. The SABC personnel officer looked me in the eyes: 'Above all what this job requires is a total commitment to the medium of television,' he said. A total commitment to the medium of television? But I had already made a total commitment – to Jesus Christ. There could be no other total commitment for me. I began to think about full time Christian ministry. It seemed clear to me that I could only give of my best to something which mattered supremely to me, above all else. I had by now discovered that following Jesus was a calling that was worthy of all my energy and dedication, indeed, of my whole life. So, one afternoon, towards the end of 1974 I went to see the Bishop-Suffragan of Natal, Bishop Ken Hallowes, about offering myself for ordination in the Anglican Church. By the end of the afternoon I had been accepted as an ordinand. The course of my future life had been set.

I went to Wycliffe Hall, Oxford, in England, for three years of theological training, and in 1978 I returned to be ordained as a deacon in the Diocese of Natal. I was appointed to serve in the parish of St. Alphege's, Scottsville, a suburb of Pietermaritzburg. This was a lively, growing church and the three years that I spent there were years of seeing God at work in many exciting and wonderful ways. During this time St. Alphege's Church was widely known as a centre of renewal, evangelism and healing ministry. It was a great privilege for me to be involved in all of this. I learned a great deal and made many good friends, and I could not have wished for a more exhilarating start to my life as an ordained minister. It was also during my time at St. Alphege's that I got married to Alison, whom I had met while

My Journey

I was at theological college in England. So it is not surprising that I look back on those three years as being very special!

However at the same time there was a growing sense of frustration and unease within me. Dating from my experience at Kentani I had been committed to what is usually called the evangelical understanding of the Christian faith. As an evangelical I believed in the particular importance of the Bible as the primary source of authority and direction for Christian life. I also believed in the need for a personal response of repentance and faith in Jesus Christ as Lord and Saviour. (These have remained as central principles for me in my Christian faith and life.) Both of these were strongly emphasized and upheld in the congregation at St. Alphege's. Because of the reputation of St. Alphege's as an 'alive' church, it had attracted many members who had little or no Anglican background, and many who had come from various Pentecostal churches or house groups. However, among a number of the people at St. Alphege's there was an unwillingness to listen to some of the things which it seemed to me God was saying about the situation in South Africa. Often, in fact, there was a downright hostility when the subject of the church and 'politics' was raised. Yet the Bible clearly had much to say about justice, about paying proper wages, about listening to the cries of the oppressed, and so on. I sensed that the Holy Spirit was speaking to the church about these issues, and yet this was being emphatically denied by many of our church members. Raising these issues seemed to be regarded as 'unspiritual' and not the mark of a true 'Bible believer'. Other issues became similarly controversial.

The issue of adult baptism versus infant baptism was one; another was the use of liturgy in church. Here was I, preparing for the role of leadership in the local church, yet I was not able to deal with such crucial issues as these, in a church which strongly emphasized the Bible as the final authority in all such matters. I was clearly out of my depth.

As a result of these problems, at the end of my time at St. Alphege's I decided to return to England for further study, rather than continuing in parish ministry in South Africa. I needed a break, a time to think through some of these issues. I wanted to look again at the Bible, at the basis of its authority in the life of the church, and to understand better how the Bible should be used in matters of faith and doctrine. I had not lost my belief in the authority of the Bible, but I had come to realize that it is not enough simply to profess obedience to the Lord Jesus Christ and to the Holy Scriptures. Many people do this and yet remain blind to those things which they simply do not wish to see. The challenge lies not so much in what we profess, but in what we are willing to do in obedience to Jesus. Jesus is the one who is at the very heart of Christianity and the Bible. Above all he asks us to be like him and to do the things that we see him doing.

He is the Word made flesh, the Messiah, the 'author and finisher' of our faith. (Heb. 12:2 KJV) Gradually I came to see that the answer to my questions lay in an uncompromising response of obedience to Jesus and to the demands of his love.

My Journey

This might be too costly for many Christians, but nonetheless, this was what he wanted from his church. Was I ready for such uncompromising obedience? I wanted to be, but I was all too conscious of my own weakness and lack of commitment.

I spent two years taking an MA degree in Biblical Studies at the University of Sheffield and at the same time I worked in a parish church in the city of Sheffield. Slowly the problems and questions of my time at St. Alphege's were resolved and answered. Then out of the blue I received a letter from the Bishop of Natal. Would I accept appointment as the new Rector of the Church of the Ascension, Hilton? My wife, Alison, and I spent some time praying and thinking about this, and soon we both felt a clear sense that this was where God wanted us to be. In August, 1983, we left Sheffield and returned to South Africa. This was to be a new challenge for me; the challenge to put into practice all that I had come to believe about the church of the Lord Jesus Christ, and in particular about the calling of the church in South Africa.

* * *

As I reflect on this story of my own seeking and finding God there are some essentials of Christian truth which have been very significant for me. Above all is my deepening awareness that I know God as a Holy Trinity, one God in three persons. This, of course, is central to all Christian doctrine. Many books have been written on the subject of the

Trinity and yet it remains a mystery, the mystery of the nature of God himself, which no human mind can fathom. But I have found, in common with millions of Christians down the ages, that I experience God in three persons. He is indisputably one God, yet he comes to me as Father, as Son and as Holy Spirit.

i) *God the Father*

I have come to know and to trust God as a loving and merciful father. My own experience of God's goodness and mercy is expressed very movingly and clearly in that most famous of the psalms, Psalm 23: 'The Lord is my shepherd, I shall not want; he makes me lie down in green pastures. He leads me beside still waters; he restores my soul.' (vv. 1–2)

I also experience many answers to my prayers, some in direct, practical ways, and others which rather reveal more of God and his ways to me. I recognize the greatness of God in creation, and in all the manifold patterns and purposes of our life here on earth. I find that in particular the psalms speak to me over and over again of these many ways in which God makes himself known as Father to those who love him and who seek him with all their heart.

ii) *God the Son*

Then I experience God in Jesus Christ his Son, God in human form, whom I know both as Lord and as Saviour. He is Lord because he is alive, risen from the dead, and he is God, one with the Father, ruling over all the universe. (Col. 1:15–17)

My Journey

He is Saviour to me because I know him to be the one who has authority on earth to forgive sins. (Mark 2:10) I do not understand fully how it came to be that 'Christ died for our sins according to the Scriptures' (1 Cor. 15:3 NIV), but there is no question that in my own experience I am set free from guilt and from the power of sin to control me, through repentance and faith in Jesus. My experience is the same as that of Paul: 'Therefore, since we are justified by faith, we have peace with God through our Lord Jesus Christ.' (Rom. 5:1)

iii) *God the Holy Spirit*

Thirdly, it is my experience that the Holy Spirit dwells in me and gives life to my mortal body, exactly as the Bible describes it: 'If the Spirit of him who raised Jesus from the dead dwells in you, he who raised Christ Jesus from the dead will give life to your mortal bodies also through his Spirit which dwells in you.' (Rom. 8:11) Jesus proclaimed: '"If any one thirst, let him come to me and drink. He who believes in me, as the scripture has said, 'Out of his heart shall flow rivers of living water.'" Now this he said about the Spirit.' (John 7:37–39)

Shortly after I had been to the Kentani Mission and had come to a decision to follow Jesus Christ as Lord I began to know the presence of the Holy Spirit in my life. I wouldn't say that the Holy Spirit had not been with me before, but I had little real awareness of him, as the third person of the Holy Trinity, living in me. However, about a month after the Kentani work camp, I was in Johannesburg and I happened to wander into the office of a Pentecostal church group in the Hillbrow area. After some discussion with the Pentecostal pastor, I was asked whether I had ever spoken in tongues. 'No,' I replied, uncertainly. He explained to me about the gift of speaking in tongues, and asked if I would like him to pray for me to receive it. 'Well,' I said, 'if it is of God, then I want it.' He had convinced me that this was worth trying at any rate, and so I knelt down with him on the floor of his office to pray.

He prayed a short prayer in English, and then started to speak in tongues aloud. It sounded to me rather like the gibberish of a child, but I joined in without any difficulty and prayed along with him for a short while. As I think back to this, it seems that there was a childlike acceptance in me that although this did seem rather strange, nonetheless there was nothing to be afraid of or concerned about, and that God really did have something for me in this.

I can remember going out into a sunny Hillbrow afternoon feeling that although there had been no flashing lights or extraordinary experiences, yet all the same something quite significant had happened to me. And from then on, God, Jesus, the Bible and the Holy Spirit all became very much more real and important in my life. The combination of a deep surrender of the will to Jesus Christ, and an openness to the power of the Holy Spirit, resulted in an extraordinary change in my life. I began to love going to church, and to Christian meetings. You couldn't keep me away! Even the old hymns that had seemed so boring before were now full of rich meaning and great joy. I re-discovered the Bible as its words leapt out at me, charged with truth and personal significance.

My Journey

I could spend a whole evening studying and meditating on the Scriptures, without any real effort at all. In particular I found that I could say from the depths of my being, 'I love you, Lord'. Being a Christian had for me been transformed from being primarily a duty, to something very similar to a love affair – a love affair with God – and I'm sure that the Holy Spirit was responsible for this.

* * *

So I believe that I can say that I know God, in and through his Son Jesus Christ, and through the indwelling power of the Holy Spirit. I have moved from having quite a lot of knowledge about God to a real measure of knowing God and knowing his strength and goodness in my daily life, though of course, I obviously cannot claim to know God exhaustively. As the Psalms remind us over and over, God is very great. (Ps. 145:3; 48:1)

God is far greater than our traditions and our doctrine, our values and ideologies. To know him is to be changed by him. That unquestionably has been my experience and yet I am only just beginning to discover what this journey means. What does God want us to become? That will be different for each and every one of us. But I do know this – that for all of us there will be the three journeys that are really one journey – the journey upward, the journey inward, and the journey outward.

What did these journeys involve for us in Hilton? What has been the result for me personally of an upward journey in which God, Father, Son and Holy Spirit have become real? I would say that the upward journey has led, for me, directly to the outward journey, and at the same time, to the inward journey. The following chapters will attempt to describe what this has meant for me and for our local church in Hilton.

CHAPTER 5
SWEETWATERS

It hasn't been easy. I soon discovered that church leadership is a costly and difficult business. I knew very well in theory what the local church should be like. Trying to put my theories and ideals into practice in the local church has been one of the more testing experiences of my life. There is much that simply has not happened, not because I did not want it to happen, but for many other reasons, some of which were within my control, and some beyond. Certainly it has not been a 'success story' in conventional terms.

Yet we as a local church have grappled with many of the crucial issues facing us. Many of us have been led into action as a result of our experience of hearing what God is saying to us about our situation. That action has meant different things for different people. But for some it has meant building relationships with people who are poor and oppressed, and learning what it is to serve the poor in the love of Jesus. As this has begun to happen, our lives have been changed. Through the poor we have come to know Jesus in new and very significant ways. We have begun to discover what the poor have to give to us, and how our lives can be enriched by obeying

Jesus' command to us to bring the good news to the poor.

When I arrived at the Church of the Ascension I soon became aware of a number of tensions in the church. The controversial departure of the previous Rector had left many people confused as to the future direction and vision for the church. During my first year therefore, I tried to clarify, in my preaching and teaching, what I believed to be the biblical vision for the local church. I also sought to bring people together and to develop a greater sense of unity in the parish. I tried, in particular, to emphasize to the congregation, that the love of Jesus should determine our priorities in the local church. In my vestry report in April 1984 I wrote:

> The ministry to Sweetwaters is, I believe, a most important dimension to our life as a parish. Through Graham Beggs and those who help and support him, we are able to be involved in the concern of the gospel for the whole of society and the whole of man's need, physical and spiritual. If we as a parish are to be true to the message of the gospel, then we must deepen our concern for, and our involvement with, those who do not share our own cultural and material inheritance, especially those who are left on the margins of society, without the power or the means which most of us have to provide for our basic needs and concerns.

It is one thing to offer people in the church a wonderful vision of Christian service and love.

Sweetwaters

It is another thing to enable them to do these things. In fact it is only the Holy Spirit who can enable us to live the life of Jesus here on earth; it is not something that is humanly possible. I was well aware that I could never in my own strength bring all of this into reality at the Church of the Ascension. Only God could do this, working through me and through others. So I made a serious effort to commit myself to prayer, and especially to praying for the church. Although it is difficult to maintain a discipline of daily prayer in a busy and demanding parish, I nonetheless persevered in this. Often on Wednesdays I would set aside the whole morning and go off to a place where no-one could find me, to pray and to seek God's will for myself and for the church.

Before I left Sheffield to come out to Hilton I had been involved in a group of clergy and leaders that used to meet regularly at St. Thomas Crookes, in Sheffield. On the last morning that I was with this group, before my departure for South Africa, the group prayed for me and for my ministry in my new parish. One prophetic word which was given to me during that time of prayer became a great help to me in my early years in Hilton. I was told that in my new church I would find people with many different agendas for me and for the church. 'Listen to me, and to my agenda' was the word of the Lord to me.

One of the groups that was very active in the parish in Hilton was often called 'the Sweetwaters group'. Sweetwaters is the large black area which directly adjoins our parish. In recent years its population has grown tremendously, yet even now few white people from Pietermaritzburg have even been there. For most it remains merely a name, as with so many other black areas and townships across South Africa. But Sweetwaters is our neighbouring community and for some years before I arrived in the parish, there had been a strong sense among some of the church people that our church must be involved in this community. But how? Where should they begin? The answer was through personal contact. This had been happening for many years in different and limited ways. At one time, in fact, baptisms and weddings of people from Sweetwaters all took place at the Church of the Ascension. But this had long since been discontinued.

In 1978, before I came to Hilton, the church had made a decision to employ Graham Beggs as a full-time Sweetwaters worker. His gifts lay in evangelism and in his extraordinary knowledge of, and love for, the Zulu people, their language and their culture. Graham began by simply going and spending much of his time in Sweetwaters, and by giving much time to prayer. Gradually he became known and accepted by the Zulu people there. He served them in many different ways, caring for the sick, the bereaved, those facing all kinds of practical difficulties, praying with them and preaching and teaching in their homes and in the churches. By the time I came to Hilton his ministry in Sweetwaters was already well established and accepted.

But in the Church of the Ascension it was a different story. There was a small group of people who had become strongly committed to Graham and to his ministry. They met regularly with him to pray, and further supported him by becoming involved in the Sweetwaters work themselves. But apart from this highly motivated group, there was little real involvement in Sweetwaters. The parish had bought a four-wheel-drive truck for the work, and the costs of both this and Graham's stipend were being paid from parish funds. I sensed that many in the church knew that what Graham was doing was right. I too felt that this was the direction in which God was calling us, as a church. Our church's finances were showing that we were trying to be obedient. Yet more than this was needed. It was not enough to leave it all to Graham and 'his group'. Many more people needed to become personally involved. Supporting the work from a distance was one thing: actually going to Sweetwaters and doing the work was a different challenge altogether.

Soon after arriving in Hilton I made arrangements to go into Sweetwaters with Graham. I didn't know what to expect. When I had asked people what Graham actually did, many had said, 'Well, I don't know what he does, but I know that God is in it.' Even Graham himself would not tell me what he did. 'Come and see,' he said. I realized later that he had by this time become frustrated with trying to explain his work to others, when the only way that people could know what it was about was by going themselves. It is not enough to know about Jesus from a distance. Like Nathanael in John Chapter 1, we have to 'Come and see'.

I sat beside Graham in the parish's Isuzu truck. We left the only major road which goes through Sweetwaters – which was itself a dirt road, full of potholes – and drove up a track in the side of a hill which could by no stretch of the imagination be called a road. I understood very quickly that the parish truck was essential if this work was to continue. If people were to have to use their private cars on these tracks they would not be likely to last very long. Not surprisingly the few cars owned by the people of Sweetwaters don't last very long either.

We visited the home of an old Zulu woman, Alice, who greeted us joyfully. Although she was very poor and lived in a small mud house with a rudimentary corrugated iron roof, the strength which came from her faith in Jesus Christ shone out of her. I could see that to her, Graham was a beloved friend, a pastor and a brother in Christ. I started to grasp that whatever others might say about Graham and his ministry, there was something here that spoke to me very clearly about Jesus himself. It was something that I myself needed to pursue and take hold of, even though I strongly suspected that it could involve the transformation of my Christian discipleship.

Graham and I went on to make other visits, to a crêche for pre-school children, and to the home of another old Zulu woman, again full of faith and joy in Christ, despite the obvious burdens of her poverty. Eventually we went home to Hilton, back from the mud and dirt of Sweetwaters to our clean comfortable homes. I was not surprised that Graham was often misunderstood by people in our church. What he was doing was so costly, so real, so clearly a reflection of much that was at the centre of Jesus' own life and ministry. I could see that it would simply not be possible for him to move easily and quietly between the white homes of Hilton and the mud huts of people like Alice. He was bound to be a disturber amongst us, a challenge to our complacency and our unwillingness to be truly changed by Jesus Christ and his love for the poor and the suffering. He was bound to bring words of confrontation to our church. Would not Jesus have done the same? Somehow, we needed to face up to what God was saying to us through Graham. Not just me and a small group of others, but the whole church, including me. This was, I knew, what was needed.

CHAPTER 6
LEARNING TO SERVE THE POOR

I began to spend more time with Graham so that I could come to a greater understanding of his work and ministry. I knew that he had much that was important to teach us, particularly about the way in which we should go about sharing the gospel with the Zulu people. Not everyone could be like Graham; he was clearly a person with special gifts and abilities. But all of us could respond to the call of Jesus for us to go in his love to the people of Sweetwaters. Graham stressed time and time again that we had to 'Go'. It was not enough to stay within the security of our own community. God was calling our church to 'Go'.

So, in a number of different ways, I sought to support Graham and to help the parish as a whole to hear what Graham and others were saying to us about Sweetwaters and about the need to 'Go'. It was a long, slow process.

In 1985 the Bishop sent Richard Shorten to work in our parish for a year. Richard was in his final year of training for ordination. He had completed most of the academic requirements for ordination, and he came to us to gain a year's practical experience in parish work. I suggested to Richard

Learning to Serve the Poor

that he should personally become involved in the Sweetwaters ministry, and should try to get more people, from a wider spectrum of the life of the parish, involved. As a result of this a number of new people were drawn in.

Gradually other areas of work also opened up. Betty Bradford with her concern for evangelism built up a number of teams of women who would go on weekday mornings and meet with groups of Zulu women in different areas of Sweetwaters. These groups focussed firstly on basic Christian teaching and on learning to pray for one another. However, an integral part of this has also been a concern for specific practical needs. These are often shared with the church in Hilton and people are encouraged to help in whatever way they can. The story of Jabu is one example of this.

Jabu was a little girl, destitute and severely handicapped, who was discovered wandering the hillsides by Mita, an elderly widow. She did not speak or respond, and was almost totally expressionless, apparently petrified. She had been rejected and abandoned by her own family because of her handicaps. Mita adopted Jabu into her own home and began to bring her to the Tuesday morning women's meeting. The women prayed for her each Tuesday, and very slowly she started to respond. Her eyes began to get brighter; she started to smile. After about a year the Lord had healed her sufficiently for us to send her to a school for handicapped children. Our Thursday congregation in Hilton were asked to take a special interest in little Jabu, to send clothing for her, to pay her school fees and to pray regularly for her. Recently we were told by the head of the school that she attends that there is every hope that Jabu will one day be able to live a normal life in society.

Every year in January and February, many Zulu people face a financial crisis because of the need to pay annual school fees, which have to be paid at the start of the school year. In Sweetwaters there are many widows and other women, with very little income, who are personally responsible for a large number of children, sometimes as many as twelve or even fifteen. Our church has for some years now assisted a number of families with these school fees. This is done through personal contact and knowledge of the circumstances of each family, and not on a 'hand-out' basis.

A problem that we often encounter in this kind of work is the language barrier. However, our experience has been that when there is a genuine desire to go and be with the people this quickly ceases to be a major problem. The knowledge of a few Zulu words and phrases, together with the help of an interpreter, is quite sufficient to begin with. Soon one picks up the language and gains confidence, and there are always Zulu people who are willing to help, to read the Bible in Zulu or to interpret a short teaching or message.

Another important development was the establishment of a Bonginkosi feeding scheme at a school in the Inadi area of Sweetwaters.

The Bonginkosi project had been developed by two Pietermaritzburg women, Barbara Davies and Daphne Tshabalala, as part of the ministry of African Enterprise, the evangelistic organisation headed by Michael Cassidy. Its primary aim was

Learning to Serve the Poor

to help feed thousands of black school children, many of whom were coming to school each day with empty stomachs. Bonginkosi began when Daphne Tshabalala, who was the principal of the large Nichols Primary School in Edendale, threw some bread crusts to a dog outside her office one morning. Before the dog could get to the crusts a child had grabbed them and run off to eat them. Daphne told Barbara Davies about this incident and so after prayer, and in response to this desperate need, Daphne and Barbara set up this feeding scheme. Churches from Pietermaritzburg were linked to black schools in the Greater Pietermaritzburg area. A partnership was entered into between the school staff and parents on the one hand, and members of the church on the other. The initial aim was to provide, free of charge, a cup of hot soup and a large chunk of bread to as many as possible of the most needy pupils at the school. This was done as an act of Christian service; Bonginkosi means, literally, 'Thank the Lord'.

Pat Caldwell, a member of our congregation, read a challenge by Michael Cassidy for Christians to become involved in action and practical service which would help to bring reconciliation and healing to South Africa. 'Do your bit,' Michael had often preached and written. 'If every Christian does their bit, South Africa will be saved.' Pat took this to heart, prayed about it and spoke to a number of people about what she personally could do in response to this challenge. The outcome was that Pat became involved in organising a group of women in setting up a Bonginkosi feeding scheme at Mbanjwa School in Sweetwaters.

This feeding scheme developed rapidly, with a group from the church going every Monday morning to take bread and soup powder and other provisions, and to meet with the staff at the school. A woman was then employed to take care of the preparation of the food, and a small room was provided for this and made secure. Before long some 500 children were being fed every day. While this was happening Pat became aware of the need of some of the mothers of the children for Christian teaching and Bible study. Soon a regular Monday morning meeting was taking place, on the grass outside the school, with twenty or thirty women coming together to sing, hear the Bible taught (through an interpreter) and to pray.

Pat knew that many of the women who came to these meetings were very poor and many were responsible for children whom they were unable to feed and clothe adequately. They were mostly unemployed, with little prospect of being able to earn any money at all. This deeply concerned her, and as she thought and prayed about it, a new idea came to her. She read Titus 3:14, 'Our people must learn to devote themselves to doing what is good, in order that they may provide for daily necessities and not live unproductive lives.' (NIV)

Pat, together with her friend Sarah Dottridge, also a member of our church, began to teach some of the women to crochet woollen blankets. With a little instruction and help, these women were soon able to produce high quality blankets, made by hand in their homes. Orders for these blankets came in steadily and there has been no

Learning to Serve the Poor

problem in finding buyers for 'Bonginkosi blankets'. They have even been exported to Canada. This blanket-making 'co-operative' is managed by the women from our church who provide the expertise to keep production going and to market the blankets. It is now based in a local church, a short distance away from the school. Each Monday there is a women's meeting at which blankets are collected, money is paid out, wool is supplied and cheap, nutritious food is available for the women to buy with their earnings. All this, however, takes place after the meeting for worship, Bible teaching and prayer, which is led both by women from Hilton and by the local women themselves. There is often opportunity for individuals with particular needs to receive prayer and ministry, perhaps for physical healing, perhaps for problems in the family or in the community.

A further development was a candle-making project, to be run on similar lines to the blanket-making, but this ran into serious practical difficulties and had to be abandoned. Some things work, and some things don't. We are learning as we go along.

It is important to see how the spiritual and the practical have come together. The needs of the people are both physical and spiritual, and the success of much of this work lies in the way in which both areas of need have been taken seriously. Christian love and care should never try to separate the spiritual needs of a person from their physical needs, or vice versa.

Pat Caldwell has set out the way in which this all works in the following diagram:

The Sweetwaters Circle of Liberating Care

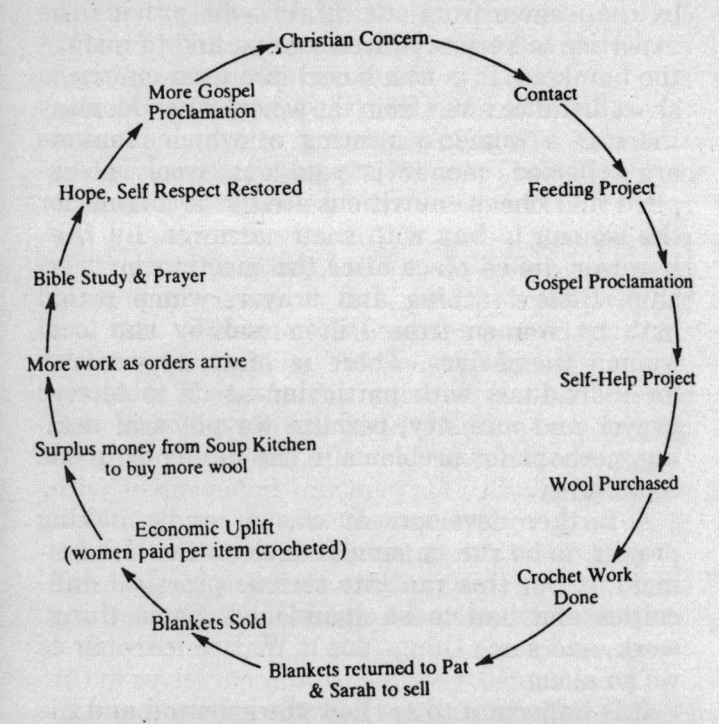

Christian Concern → Contact → Feeding Project → Gospel Proclamation → Self-Help Project → Wool Purchased → Crochet Work Done → Blankets returned to Pat & Sarah to sell → Blankets Sold → Economic Uplift (women paid per item crocheted) → Surplus money from Soup Kitchen to buy more wool → More work as orders arrive → Bible Study & Prayer → Hope, Self Respect Restored → More Gospel Proclamation → Christian Concern

The principles which lie behind the Bonginkosi work are applied throughout our whole Sweetwaters ministry. The leaders of the different Sweetwaters groups meet regularly to share what is happening, to pray for one another and to encourage one another. Some are involved with a crêche, others with church groups, giving teaching and encouragement, while others are seeking to evangelize and to disciple new converts. Last year one group was able to arrange for two local people to be trained as sewing instructors, and they are now teaching others to sew and to make clothes in Sweetwaters itself. It is clear that this varied ministry has proved wonderfully fruitful, and hundreds of lives have been positively affected through the love of Christ at work in his people.

There are those in our church who for one reason or another are not able to go into Sweetwaters regularly. However, we encourage as many as possible to go, even if it is only occasionally. We have to start where we are, with whatever it is that we have to offer. But it is very important that we offer something of ourselves, and not simply give of our surplus of material wealth, without any personal involvement. We believe that the way of Jesus is the way of love and servanthood, not the way of handouts which pass the responsibility for personal involvement with the poor on to someone else.

From this flows a key principle which I have learnt in particular from Graham Beggs, and which we have tried to uphold and teach in all our Sweetwaters ministry. This is that we need first and foremost to be willing to offer ourselves in the service of Christ, rather than offering our material gifts. It is one thing to bring some old clothes or a packet of mealie meal or powdered milk, and to leave it at the parish office for someone else to distribute. It is another thing entirely to be willing to go to Sweetwaters, not with material gifts but to go empty-handed; to go simply to meet the people, to be with them, to share their lives and to slowly build relationships based on mutual respect and truth. Then, in due time, with those who are our fellow-Christians, we are able to pray together, to sing and worship together, to study the Bible together, and to give of ourselves to one another in all sorts of ways.

When one of the women of our church was considering how to become involved in helping with a crêche in Sweetwaters, she asked me, 'But, how do I begin?' I said, 'Just go empty-handed, and say, "If there is anything I can help you with, please let me know." Try to go regularly, and to take an interest in the crêche, try to make friends with the principal and the teachers, and I'm sure that God will soon show you the way forward.' She did this and slowly a relationship of trust and openness developed.

Perhaps one of the main reasons why serving the poor is so hard for many of us is that it involves accepting the way of the cross. The way of the cross is the way of humility, of emptying ourselves, of laying down our lives for one another. The cross cuts right across our human pride, our desire to hold on to and to be held in esteem for what we are and what we have. It is a direct rebuke to our society's preoccupation with name, position and wealth. In Philippians 2:5–11, we read of Christ's example which led him in obedience to death on a cross.

> Have this mind among yourselves, which is yours in Christ Jesus, who, though he was in the form of God, did not count equality with God a thing to be grasped, but emptied himself, taking the form of a servant, being born in the likeness of men. And being found in human form he humbled himself and became obedient unto death, even death on a cross. Therefore God has highly exalted him and

Learning to Serve the Poor

bestowed on him the name which is above every name, that at the name of Jesus every knee should bow, in heaven and on earth and under the earth, and every tongue confess that Jesus Christ is Lord, to the glory of God the Father.

It has become clear to me that one of the most important ways in which Christians are called by Jesus to follow his example of humility and of self-emptying is in serving the poor. This is an essential aspect of Christian discipleship. It is also one that has been greatly neglected by much of the western church. If the western church is to have a biblical integrity in its mission and in its witness to the world, it must be seen to be serving the poor, the outcasts, the lepers and the prostitutes, as Jesus himself did. In an interview in *Melody Maker*, December 19/26 1987, Bono, the lead singer in the Irish rock group U2 said,

> I'd say that, if Jesus Christ was on earth you'd probably find him in a gay bar in San Francisco. He'd be working with people suffering from Aids. These people are the new lepers. Just like the turn of BC/AD — don't touch them, walk away from them. If you want to find out where Jesus would be hanging out, it'll always be with the lepers.

Of course Jesus also spent time with the rich young ruler, he met with Nicodemus who was a ruler of the Jews, and he ate at the house of Simon the Pharisee. But he showed a particular concern for the poor, the lepers, the cripples, the blind and the lame. There is so much in the Gospels which speaks about this. For example in Luke 14:12–14 we read,

> He said also to the man who had invited him, 'When you give a dinner or a banquet, do not invite your friends or your brothers or your kinsmen or rich neighbours, lest they also invite you in return, and you be repaid. But when you give a feast, invite the poor, the maimed, the lame, the blind, and you will be blessed, because they cannot repay you. You will be repaid at the resurrection of the just.'

Jesus is speaking here about the importance of giving without expecting any reward, and about the need to be unconditionally generous and good, just as our heavenly Father is towards us. But this passage is also a powerful rebuke to the priorities of much of modern Christianity.

What a challenge it is for any local church today to put this bit of Jesus' teaching into practice.

There is also the description of the last judgment, in Matthew 25:31–46. We are told that the King will say to the righteous,

> 'Come, O blessed of my Father, inherit the kingdom prepared for you from the foundation of the world; for I was hungry and you gave me food, I was thirsty and you gave me drink, I was a stranger and you welcomed me, I was naked and you clothed me, I was sick and you visited me, I was in prison and you came to me.' Then the righteous will answer him, 'Lord, when did we see thee hungry . . .'

Learning to Serve the Poor

> And the King will answer them, 'Truly I say to you, as you did it to one of the least of these my brethren, you did it to me.'

The test of the authenticity of our faith in Christ lies in whether or not we are obedient to his commands. Jesus said, 'You are my friends if you do what I command you'. (John 15:14) 'Faith apart from works is dead,' says the letter of James. (James 2:26) Jesus clearly understood that acts of mercy and caring for the stranger, the homeless, the hungry, the sick and those in prison would be present in the lives of those who belong to his Kingdom. Jesus said, 'A new commandment I give to you, that you love one another; even as I have loved you, that you also love one another.' (John 13:34) Obedience to Jesus is primarily obedience to his commandment to love one another as he has loved us. This is the test of our discipleship. 'By this all men will know that you are my disciples, if you have love for one another.' (John 13:35) We are to love our neighbour as we love ourselves, to do unto others as we would have them do to us. The gospel, in a word, is Love.

The parable of the good Samaritan (Luke 10:25–37) was told in reply to the question, 'And who is my neighbour?' The answer that Jesus gave tells us that we will be a neighbour to anyone who is in need of our help, if we have mercy on them.

To be faithful in our Christian discipleship we must, each one of us, ask, 'Who is my neighbour?' If we are sincere in our asking, we will not have to look very far to discover the answer. Our neighbour may be poor, and he or she may be rich. But there will always be a cost in showing mercy to our neighbour. There was a cost in time, in money, and in personal involvement for the good Samaritan. Besides which, he was a Samaritan. He was not a socially or religiously acceptable person in Jewish eyes. Jesus often calls us to cross cultural, racial and religious barriers in showing mercy; and this also is costly.

If the church is not faithful in this aspect of discipleship, then the integrity of our claim to be serving Jesus Christ as Lord is called into question. The world watches the church to see whether it truly has something to offer to meet the need of the world. The church is judged principally by its deeds, not by its words. Words have become cheap but deeds are costly. 'Be doers of the word, and not hearers only, deceiving yourselves,' says the letter of James. (James 1:22)

Jackie Pullinger is an Englishwoman who works with the poor, the drug addicts and the prostitutes in the Walled City of Hong Kong. I was fortunate to hear her speak a few years ago at Holy Trinity Church, Brompton, in London. She spoke very movingly about what it means to share God's heart for the poor and for the unlovely. She reminded us of the words sent to John the Baptist, when he was in prison and was asking whether Jesus was indeed the Messiah. Jesus said to the disciples of John, 'Go and tell John what you hear and see: the blind receive their sight and the lame walk, lepers are cleansed and the deaf hear, and the dead are raised up, and the poor have good news preached to them.' (Matt. 11:4–5) Jackie Pullinger said that when people see these things happening, many will recognize that Jesus is truly

Learning to Serve the Poor

the Messiah. There in Holy Trinity, Brompton, she asked people who were willing to ask God to give them a heart for the poor to come forward so that she and her team could pray for them. Many came forward that night to be prayed for by Jackie and her team of former heroin addicts from the Walled City. Surely God is seeking those in the church in South Africa who are willing also for him to give them a heart for the poor.

In *Renewal* magazine of August, 1987, Jackie Pullinger wrote:

> We have to share the love of God with the poor, oppressed and hurting people. We have to go down the streets and give, as he told us to, his peace to the poor. We have to share our rice box with the hungry, our blanket with the cold. The hungry people in the world are our responsibility. The money we have, the land we have, the life we have, are not ours. What made us think we were owners? We are to bless the poor, the hungry, the oppressed.

In South Africa the church faces a great challenge, because all around us there are poor, suffering, deprived and oppressed people. Where do we begin to serve the poor? We can begin by asking, 'Who is my neighbour?' When God shows us who our neighbour is, we can ask him for strength to love and serve that person. It is important that we are not so overwhelmed by the magnitude of the need that we give up even before we have begun. We must begin with people, individual people whom we can get to know and care about and serve. We see in the Gospels how Jesus met with many different people and ministered to each one personally and individually, according to their particular need. This was his way, and it should be ours too. We are his body here on earth, his hands, his feet, his eyes. We have to reach out to one another, and touch one another with his love.

> Christ
> has no
> body now on earth but ours,
> no hands but ours,
> no feet but ours.
>
> Ours are the eyes through
> which must look out Christ's
> compassion on the world.
>
> Ours are the feet with which
> He is to go about doing good.
>
> Ours are the hands with which
> He is to bless men now.
>
> St. Teresa

CHAPTER 7
THE FLOODS

South Africa is a dramatic land. My wife, Alison, sometimes smiles when people say that South Africa is not really a wild place. She will tell you that in our time at Hilton we have experienced a tornado, forest fire, earthquake (tremor, anyway), flood and civil war, all within our immediate local area.

The year 1987 will go down in the history of Natal as the year of the floods. It began raining on Friday, September 25th. It rained all day Saturday, and again all day Sunday. On Monday the rain was still coming down hard. Flood warnings started to be issued, but no one was prepared for what was to happen. By Monday afternoon there was already widespread damage. Major bridges were being washed away. Accurate information as to which roads were still open was difficult to come by. Towards the end of the 8 p.m. news on television the announcers said that they had received a report that the giant John Ross bridge over the Tugela River – the main link between Durban and Zululand – had been washed away, and that a number of vehicles had been on the bridge when it collapsed. It rained all Monday night. I can still remember the sound of the rain that night, no longer welcome or life-giving, but now life-destroying, frightening and unstoppable.

On Tuesday morning the rain did at last stop. Gradually the scale of the disaster became clear. All over Natal roads and houses, even factories, had been washed away. Thousands upon thousands had been left homeless. A massive flood relief operation began to get underway.

On the Tuesday, Graham Beggs went to Sweetwaters to see the situation there. The reports that he brought back were alarming. In whole areas, houses had been washed away. The houses are made mainly of mud, and are only able to resist a certain amount of heavy rain, before they begin to crumble and fall apart. A few days later I went with Graham to see for myself. The damage was appalling. Many houses had partially collapsed, and many were largely roofless. We went into some of the homes. In one everything had been soaked. Most of the furniture was ruined. The beds, the clothes, everything was in a total mess. What it must have been like for them that Monday night I could not imagine. I had found it frightening, and I lived in a strong house with a safe roof over my head.

What happened next was not really planned; it just happened. All over Natal flood relief programmes were being organised. We had a meeting to plan our response in Hilton, but the scale of the needs was so vast that we did not know what would be involved. However, certain priorities were established. First of all food was needed to reach those who had lost all their food supplies. Clothing and blankets were also a priority, especially as there was the threat of

The Floods

further heavy rain. Financial assistance and the rebuilding of homes would be the second phase. A fund run through the Church of the Ascension would be started specifically to help.

Food started to pour in. Various businesses and factories gave large quantities of mealie meal, longlife milk and other supplies. Some of it was already packaged, some was in bulk and needed to be weighed out and put into bags. A roster was drawn up for the use of the Sweetwaters truck. Each day virtually from dawn to dusk the truck travelled in and out of Sweetwaters, ferrying supplies to those in need. Graham Beggs worked tirelessly, going himself, and enabling others to reach those who were in the most need. His knowledge of the area, and the infrastructure of relationships which people of the church had built up over the years, meant that we were able to be effective in bringing outside help into the Sweetwaters area in these circumstances, and see that it actually reached the people who were in greatest need.

The Sunday after the floods many churches in different parts of South Africa made appeals for food, clothing and money to be sent to Natal as flood relief. A large Baptist church in Johannesburg, collected a whole ten ton containerload of clothing, bedding and other gifts. Colin Bishop, the pastor of a Baptist Church in Johannesburg, phoned Michael Cassidy to ask whether he knew of an appropriate organisation to which this container could be sent. The church was particularly concerned that their gifts should be distributed through a Christian agency or church, so that in some way the comfort and love of Christ would be conveyed to those who received them. Michael suggested that the container be sent to the Church of the Ascension. On the Tuesday evening, it arrived in Hilton. The word had been sent out and many people arrived at the church to help unpack the container. The quantity of gifts was enormous! We took about two hours to unload it, with men, women, and young people forming human chains to pass things from one to another, out of the truck, across the church courtyard and into the hall. Eventually it was all unpacked, and the truck left. We went and gazed at the state of our church hall. It was piled literally to the roof with clothes, shoes, blankets, coats, all in a complete jumble. I could not even walk into the hall. I could only stand at the door and gape.

Another roster was needed. This time it was for those who would be willing to help with sorting. Children's jerseys, clothes, food, bedding and so on all needed to be sorted and put into the right pile and box so that it could later be taken out and given to the appropriate people in Sweetwaters. The task of faithfully distributing such a huge quantity of gifts was daunting. Virtually the whole church seemed to be mobilized by the urgency of the needs and the scale of the task. People worked all day, some for an hour or two, others working all through the day, and well into the night, to sort, pack and distribute. Not only the church hall, but all the other rooms that were available were piled high. Even my Rector's office became a food storeroom. Eventually after two or three weeks I was able to clear a way through the packets of mealie meal and milk powder, and actually sit down at my desk again!

The Floods

In retrospect, I see what happened as a miracle. God used a group of people who were available, and who had been prepared over many years for just such an operation, to bring relief and comfort to thousands of people in their time of suffering. Our church was not unique in this. Many churches, and other organisations, were involved in similar operations in other areas. But Sweetwaters was the area that God had given to us to reach and be involved in. I was deeply grateful to God for what I saw happening in and through our church during those days.

I have to acknowledge also that my own first reaction, when Graham started to tell me of the scale of the needs in Sweetwaters, was to think, 'Oh no! I don't want to be involved in this.' I suspect that many might have a similar response to a situation of vast and very demanding human need. But soon I saw the needs for myself, and together with many others, I got caught up in doing what needed to be done. Ordinary daily routines and the normal life of the parish had to give way. Something more important was happening.

The needs in Sweetwaters were not simply material needs. One family that I visited were clearly in a state of shock and numbness, a couple of days after the flood was over. Their house was largely ruined, their possessions badly damaged. Much of their clothing had even been washed away down the valley and was gone for ever. I had never realised how much damage water could do to a wooden sideboard, or a piece of carpet. The faces of some of the people were expressionless; acceptance was only slowly beginning to sink in. Others started to cry as we met with them and spoke to them. With some we were then able to pray together that they would know the comfort of God. We prayed with them there in the ruins of their homes that God would be their helper and their strength.

Gradually the food and clothing mountains disappeared, until there were only a few piles of remnants. The immediate need for relief in the form of food and warm clothing was largely over. It was time to move into the second phase, which chiefly meant the rebuilding of houses. Considerable sums of money had been donated to the Sweetwaters Relief Fund, and we eventually had over R25,000 available, mainly for repairs, and rebuilding. Graham worked out a system whereby a team of four or five men could, over two days, put up the basic structure for new houses, including the roof. Filling in all the walls and putting in windows and doors would then follow later. This simple basic structure cost R1,000 each. Therefore we were in a position to rebuild twenty-five homes. We started to organise teams to go to Sweetwaters, preferably working with the local people on this rebuilding programme. One group was made up of team members of African Enterprise. They decided at short notice to cancel two days of their staff retreat and instead go to Sweetwaters to build a house. While they were doing this, some of the local Zulu people came up to talk to them. They were asked who they were, and why they were doing this. When it was explained that they were doing this because they were Christians, one man said, 'If this is what Christians do, then I want to be a Christian.'

There were other aspects to our involvement.

The Floods

Many Zulu people came to us for help in applying for financial assistance from the State flood relief fund, as well as from their employers. The church became known to the Sweetwaters people as the place to go for help. For a while there were large numbers of Zulu people arriving at the church in Hilton each day hoping to be given free food and clothes. Very quickly we became aware of the problems that this could cause, and told the people that we would only be giving out food and clothes in Sweetwaters itself. However, there were bound to be exceptions to the rule, and we tried to recognize those individuals who were in genuine need, who came sometimes long distances from Sweetwaters to receive assistance from us.

There were many lessons for us in all of this. We saw how, in the face of a major disaster, the privileged white community could rise to the challenge of coming to the assistance of the stricken black community. We could not simply leave it to somebody else. Emergency services virtually do not operate in Sweetwaters, but even if they had done, the scale of the disaster was far too great for them to have been able to cope on their own.

However, I had to recognize that even in a natural disaster like this, the social and political realities of South Africa were at work. The privileged community are those who have the means and resources to build houses which can withstand rain and flood. The poor are those who always seem to suffer, because they do not have the resources or the power to protect themselves. Again there is a profound challenge for the church in this.

Our flood relief effort was a kind of 'ambulance

ministry', bringing aid in a time of emergency. But floods could happen again, and unless something were done on the political and social levels, the same people would always be the ones to suffer. So the issues needed to be faced on a number of different levels; the individual people, the local community, and the provincial and national government. Clearly the church as a whole needs to be involved at every level. But even the local church needs to recognize the full range of issues, and to take them seriously, despite their complexity and very considerable challenge.

In particular, the floods brought home to me that the years of quiet working to develop the Sweetwaters ministry had produced something very significant, a foundation of relationships and resources which was able to make a major contribution in this time of crisis. In this disaster a group of ordinary people were enabled to serve God, by his grace, and to his glory, as many hundreds received in a small way an assurance of the care of others and the care of God himself for them. At this level and with the urgency of this crisis, we were able to make ourselves available, and the local church became an effective instrument in bringing help to those who were suffering.

So the crisis of the flood was something that our church was able to respond to reasonably well. Within a few months the crisis was over, and by and large the floods were only a memory. But shortly after the floods a new crisis began to emerge in Sweetwaters, totally different in its nature, and far more difficult to respond to. This was the beginning of the Natal violence.

Part Two

A PEOPLE OF HOPE

Part Two

A PEOPLE OF HOPE

CHAPTER 8
THE VIOLENCE AND SUFFERING

Soon after the flood disaster, we began to notice that something new was happening in Sweetwaters. Until this time Sweetwaters had been a quiet, reasonably 'safe' area. There had been considerable unrest and violence in other areas of the country, which had resulted in the first and second States of Emergency (1985 and 1986). But Sweetwaters seemed very much under the control of the traditional Zulu tribal authorities, and there was no sign of any political disturbance in this area. Late in 1987, while the flood relief work was still going on, one group of women from our church was meeting with a group of Zulu women in a village high up on one of the hillsides. While they were there a minibus came up the track that led to the village, and stopped. A number of black youths got out, came up to the village and began handing out pamphlets. Our group watched what was happening; they were not too sure what to make of this. It was not something which we had experienced before.

What was happening was that a process of politicization was beginning, spreading from the urban centres of Durban and Pietermaritzburg, out into the rural and semi-rural black areas. These areas, like Sweetwaters, had very little history or experience of any kind of overt political activity. The old tribal structures and authorities still held sway, even though they were often inefficient and sometimes even corrupt. However, many young people were now questioning these authorities, and were rapidly being mobilized by a very different vision of society, based upon the policies and views of the organizations such as the UDF (United Democratic Front), Cosatu (Congress of South African Trades Unions) and ANC (African National Congress). The result of the arrival of this new political vision was to be explosive for the whole Sweetwaters community, as indeed it has been for many other areas in Natal. In Sweetwaters there were simply none of the normal channels which are found in western democracies through which the interaction of sharply differing political viewpoints can take place. Children do not join debating societies at school in order to learn how to debate issues of conscience and belief. There are no newspapers, no means of access to the media, no elected town councils. There are virtually no roads, no school halls, recreation facilities, street lights or police stations. There is almost none of the basic infrastructure which enables a normal western society to function smoothly and democratically.

What happened in Sweetwaters was that this ideological conflict almost immediately turned into a violent struggle for political supremacy. As far as we were able to assess the situation, both sides were guilty of provocation and actual deeds of violence. The first time we heard the

The Violence and Suffering

name Sweetwaters mentioned on the national news on the radio in the police unrest report was in January 1988. We hoped that this was just an isolated incident, and that it would soon blow over. We were wrong. Very quickly, within a matter of a few months, Sweetwaters became one of the most badly affected 'areas of unrest' in the whole country.

There is much that has now been written about this civil war in Natal, for that is what it has been. Up to the time of writing, over 6,000 people have died in Natal alone. The violence has spread to other parts of the country, and at times it has threatened to derail the whole process of change and reform in South Africa. In January, 1991, the ANC and Inkatha finally worked out a major peace agreement and their leaders, Nelson Mandela and Chief Buthelezi met together and called for an end to the violence. However a culture of violence has now become embedded in much of our society. There has been a tendency for the three main players in the conflict – Inkatha, the UDF/ANC, and the S.A. Police – to spend much time blaming the others for what has been happening. It is, of course, far more constructive to try to set about dealing with one's own areas of weakness than to continually point the finger of blame elsewhere. Unfortunately it is only in recent times that this lesson seems to have been learned by the three parties involved. During 1988 and 1989 one of the most distressing aspects of the violence was the unwillingness and apparent inability of anyone to do anything significant to stop the ever widening circle of killing and destruction.

The causes of the violence are not difficult to

find. Anyone who is familiar with the conditions in areas like Sweetwaters will be able to recognize much of the reason for what has happened. The violence has to be understood in the context of the poverty and the appalling social conditions which have to a large extent been brought about by the system of apartheid. It has been estimated that 350,000 people live in the black townships of Pietermaritzburg, including shack dwellers.

Let me try and summarize the conditions these people live in:

1. An average of eleven people occupy each house, almost all houses being one or two-roomed.
2. Most of the houses are of poor quality and very few have electricity.
3. In many areas residents use communal taps and latrines.
4. Roads are poor, where there are roads.
5. Health services are inadequate.
6. Education is of a poor standard.
7. There are few if any recreational facilities in most areas.

In addition to the appalling living conditions, there is desperate financial poverty.

Investigations suggest that there is on average one breadwinner for every fifteen people, and that these people earn on average R150 to R200 per month (1987 figures).

According to the minimum 'living levels' calculated by the Bureau of Market Research at the University of Stellenbosch, it was estimated that in

1987, 70 per cent of people in the Pietermaritzburg townships were living below the breadline.[1]

There is clearly a close relationship between unemployment, poverty and violence. For young people, in particular, an intense frustration results from very poor educational opportunities, together with little prospect of any rewarding job in the future. There seems in these circumstances to be no real hope of making any worthwhile contribution to society, and so a 'nothing to lose' mentality takes over. This leads easily to crime, violence and political radicalism. Yunus Carrim, a sociologist and Natal Indian Congress executive member has said: 'People simply do not have the basic material conditions to live humanly, and in their frustration and outrage they hit out at each other instead of the system, which is more difficult to attack.'[2]

Kevin Hojem, president of the Durban Metropolitan Chamber of Commerce wrote in the *Sunday Tribune* special report, 'Towards the New Natal' that the violence should not be seen in isolation.

> It is in fact a manifestation of a crisis brought about by past government policies across the whole spectrum of human activity and endeavour, land ownership, education, economic opportunity and political participation in the running of the country.[3]

Thus, the two major causes of the violence were the ideological and political struggle between Inkatha and the UDF/ANC and the socio-economic deprivation which has largely resulted from the apartheid system.

However, there were many other contributing factors. One of the most serious was the large-scale failure of the police and the agencies of law enforcement to apprehend perpetrators of violence. In May, 1990 the Democratic Party regional director, Mr Radley Keys, gave an address to the Southern African Society of Journalists Annual Congress in Pietermaritzburg. He said that in almost three years of protracted violence in the Natal Midlands, there had been about 1,800 reported and recorded cases of murder. The number of convictions for murder in our courts numbered, at most, ten.[4] He went on to say:

> The courts operate to ensure that our rights are protected. The following facts point to a severe breakdown in the judicial system: as mentioned above, we have not been able to trace more than 10 cases where there have been convictions for murder (remembering that there have been over 1,800 murders). Also, cases that reach the courts take exceedingly long to reach the actual trial day, thus giving the accused time to either intimidate witnesses or eliminate them; and prosecutors are poorly prepared for the seriousness of the cases they have to prosecute while defence counsels are prepared thoroughly over the months of adjournments.
>
> Consequently there is breakdown of confidence in the impartiality of the police force and a total lack of credibility in the courts' ability to ensure that justice is done. This is a breakdown in law and order – nothing less.

The Violence and Suffering

This led to a breakdown of confidence not only in the forces of law and order but in the whole system of justice in society. People felt that no-one would protect them and no-one would deal with those who were doing the killing, so inevitably they would then take the law into their own hands. Revenge killings became commonplace. Families within a single community would be pitted against one another, sometimes because of the deeds of one member of one family group, perhaps a young man, a brother, a son, even a cousin. Retribution would be taken against the family and their home, and not simply against the individual concerned. And so the vicious cycle would continue.

Although the role of the police in the conflict was often controversial, it is also true that the police on a number of occasions saved many lives in extremely difficult circumstances. One such occasion was the 'battle of Nxamalala' in Sweetwaters in February, 1990. The report in *The Natal Witness* of 14th February, 1990 read:

> A three day running battle in the Sweetwaters area culminated in a siege of Nxamalala early yesterday morning, with a predominately UDF occupied territory boxed in on all sides by three groups of vigilantes.
>
> Police reported that they had battled in thick mist and mountainous terrain to disperse the fighting groups. Police spokesman, Major Pieter Kitching said riot unit members walked on foot at about 10 a.m. into the midst of the battle, with fog reducing visibility.

Before the police contingent arrived, fourteen houses had already been set alight and two people reportedly killed – one from each side.

It is one thing to read about the causes and to quote statistics in a conflict such as this. It is another thing entirely to share personally in the suffering of those involved. For me, the years 1988 and 1989 were extremely painful and harrowing, because of what I knew was happening day by day, week by week, just a few miles away in Sweetwaters. I found that I could only take in so much, and then I had to turn my attention away, because it was too much to bear. Day by day, the killings, the burning of houses, the threats and the destruction went on. No-one seemed able or willing, to stop it. I felt a sense of powerlessness and deep anger at the way in which this horrific situation was being allowed to develop, destroying and uprooting the lives of thousands of people.

There is so much more that could be said, so many stories that could, and should, be told. I would like simply to tell a few of my own stories. In South Africa during this time I became aware of a terrible disintegration of the fabric of our society. Many of those whose lives were lived out only in the so-called white areas were not clearly aware of this, but even here there was a widespread sense of unease and anxiety. But for those who took the trouble to see at first hand the effects of the violence in and around Pietermaritzburg, there could be no escaping the frightening reality. Hideous crimes were being committed many times over, and the forces of

The Violence and Suffering

law and order appeared helpless to maintain the basic standards of justice and normal community life.

Early in 1988 I went with Graham Beggs and Bishop Michael Nuttall to an area in Sweetwaters where every house was either boarded up and deserted or had been attacked and set on fire. In the midst of this eerie absence of any sign of life there was one house where people were still living. The house belonged to an old widow, Aunty Mita, very poor in material terms, but strong and vigorous in her faith in Jesus Christ. She told us how one night when gangs of youths were attacking the houses around her, she had gathered her family together in the central room and they had prayed on their knees for God's protection while stones hit the roof above them. God had indeed protected them. Their house was still intact and no-one from that family had been harmed. Why was she still there, when everyone else had fled for their lives? God had not told her to move, she said. He would be her protection and she trusted in him. The simplicity and faith and even joy in Jesus Christ of someone as poor and humanly weak as Aunty Mita was deeply moving and challenging. I thought to myself, how would I react if I had to go through what she has gone through? Would I still be living in my house, with my family, saying, as Aunty Mita said, 'Thank you, Lord, for your goodness and love and power in saving me and my family from the powers of evil. I will not move away, because God is my protector.'

* * *

From my diary: 18th September, 1988.

Today I am going into Sweetwaters with a small group of women from our church. They spend one morning a week visiting a school and a church in this area. They are involved in various community projects, a school feeding scheme and a blanket-making home industry and they also meet every week with a large group, mainly of women, for worship, prayer, encouragement and teaching.

Today, as usual, we are graphically reminded of the turmoil and violence which has taken hold of this area. We pass a number of houses which have been deserted by their occupants, who have fled to safer, quieter areas. Most have had the corrugated iron removed from the roofs, many have no windows, some are blackened from having been set on fire. Fear has gripped the people. Instead of seeing many people walking round and going about their daily business, the area is strangely quiet. People are staying in their houses, afraid to wander about freely. We stop at a pre-school crêche with which our church has been involved for many years. The principal of the crêche tells us that there has been terrible violence in that very area the previous afternoon. Four people were murdered in their homes by groups of youths, after a mass meeting had been held nearby. What can I say to her? The situation is out of control. 'We are very sad about what is happening,' I say. 'We are praying for you all.'

We go on to the school. The facilities are

appalling for a school of 400 children. There used to be more children but many have been removed from the area by their parents because of the violence. A new classroom section has been standing half built for years, with the walls only four or five feet above the ground. The new window-frames, still without glass, are rusting in half-built frames where they have been left, because the money for building has run out. In the classrooms, children, dressed often in clothes that are little more than rags, sit, many on the floor, while teachers conduct classes with only the most basic of educational aids. I am reminded that in Hilton a superb new junior school, costing hundreds of thousands of rands is at present being built for white children. The difference in priorities in government spending is clearly apparent.

When our visit to the school is over, we drive on to the church where the blanket-making enterprise is based. This has proved a marvellous way for many women to earn extra income, using their own skills. The blankets are beautifully made and the demand for them has exceeded all our expectations. It is wonderful to see how a good idea, put into practice with love, care and diligence, can make a real difference to the lives of many people.

Some time is spent collecting newly-made blankets and paying the women who have made them. Then we all meet together in the church. There are many women, some children, a few men. The Zulu singing, as usual, is beautiful and rich and full of life. I give a talk on heaven. It is a repeat of a recent family service sermon, with plenty of illustrations and visual aids. The congregation are very responsive and follow closely everything I say. At the end we ask anyone who would like us to pray for them to come forward. The whole congregation, without exception, rise up and throng to the front of the small church. Such is the sense of need among the people. We first pray for them all together, and then break into small groups to pray for individuals. Eventually they are all back in their seats and we conclude with a final chorus, during which every person present comes to shake my hand and the hands of every one of the group of women from Hilton. It has been a memorable morning.

* * *

Three days later I phoned one of the women who had been into Sweetwaters with us that Monday morning. She told me that the son of one of the Zulu women, a regular member of the group that meet with us in that church, was shot dead in cold blood outside their home in Sweetwaters the previous evening. The reason apparently was that he had refused to belong to any political organisation, either UDF or Inkatha. They are a devout Christian family, and this young man had apparently said that his allegiance was to 'church', not to Inkatha or UDF. And on Monday I had been speaking to the women's group about heaven, saying heaven is the true home of every Christian. In heaven, I had said, there is no more

The Violence and Suffering

crying and pain. In heaven there are no more guns and knives.

We must not try to minimize the realities of evil in this world, and the need for us to resist it. But a sermon about heaven is very relevant in a community where people are being mercilessly killed, and where human life has become very cheap indeed.

CHAPTER 9
THE RESPONSE OF WHITE CHRISTIANS

One Sunday afternoon in March, 1988 I joined a large group of white Christians who met with a smaller group of black Christians in the Machibise Methodist Church in Edendale. The meeting had been called by African Enterprise and IDAMASA (The Interdenominational African Ministers Association of South Africa), to pray for the situation in Pietermaritzburg and the townships in the Pietermaritzburg area. It was a hot March afternoon and in many ways we were reminded of the difference between meeting in the townships and meeting in a white area. One member of our church had not one, but two, punctures resulting from the fearsome potholes on the road to Edendale. When we came out of the meeting we found that someone had tried to steal the roof-rack off our car – in broad daylight, right outside the church!

The meeting was opened by the chairman of IDAMASA, a black Presbyterian minister, who told us that he had that day received news that his son had disappeared and so he would not be able to stay for the meeting because he had to go and be with his family. During the meeting

The Response of White Christians

Michael Cassidy spoke from Romans chapter 8. He said that the only answer to the law of sin and death in South Africa is the superior law of the Spirit of life in Christ Jesus. 'We in South Africa in 1988, like St. Paul, find that we do not know how to pray as we ought, and we need the Spirit himself to intercede for us with sighs too deep for words.' And Michael reminded us that in everything God works for good with those who love him. He said that we should remember that 'God is greater' (1 John 3:20) than what is going on around us.

I felt that it was a good and valuable meeting, certainly for the white Christians present. With Michael Cassidy, we shared the belief that prayer is powerful and that although many things needed to be done in this situation, all must flow from prayer. So for white and black Christians to be meeting together in the townships to pray in this way was something significant. But at the same time this was but a very tentative movement by comparatively few white Christians towards their fellow Christians in the townships. Our response to the violence seemed deeply inadequate, and in retrospect I know that this was true, certainly of myself and of almost all white Christians in Pietermaritzburg. Nonetheless a few individuals worked heroically and sacrificially to be with those who were suffering, and to try to bring about some measure of justice and peace-keeping within the black communities. One such group was the Imbali Support Group, which was formed during this time. They were a group of white Christians who regularly went and stayed overnight in the Imbali area near Pietermaritzburg to monitor the situation and to attempt, by their presence, to bring about a greater accountability from the authorities for what was happening. This courageous solidarity with those who were suffering proved very costly. They faced numerous threats, and their motives were often misrepresented and some even had their property vandalized and suffered physical harm.

A worker for PACSA (Pietermaritzburg Agency for Christian Social Awareness), Monika Wittenberg, was involved in a serious motor accident. She later described what happened:

> This year my birthday started with the news that Baba Gabela, father of my foster son, Sipho, had been killed on his way to work. He leaves his wife and eight children, five of whom are still dependent. As mostly happens, nobody has been arrested so far. We had not been at the house of bereavement for long, when two Riot Police vans drove up and heavily-armed police searched house and people for arms, they were all neighbours who had come to commiserate. Not even a knife was found. To cut a long story short, the youngest sister Buhle of nine years was shivering unceasingly with fear and shock. Since the age of five she has had to endure severe shocks with several attacks on the house and on Sipho. I took her home to get her out of that traumatic situation for a while. Later she was joined by her two younger brothers.
>
> On 20th June at lunchtime, I took the three children home because I had booked a midnight flight to Cape Town for Friday

22 to visit our two daughters there. I told the mother that I would not be at the funeral. Something made me say, 'Please watch me get out of Imbali safely.' (Since I had received a death threat earlier, I was in a hurry to get home.) On the way home I noticed that I was doing 70 km.p.h. I forced myself to slow down and that's what saved my life. Suddenly I had a huge police Casspir before me, driving at high speed and crossing the main artery road without stopping. Had I not slowed down, I would have been ploughed under in front of the beast. So I hit the wheel, was lifted up and thrown around at ninety degrees. It took them about another ten metres before they stopped. I thought my hour had come and committed my life into God's hands, but it seems God wants me around a bit longer! I never lost consciousness for a minute and was quite in control of the situation. I even had my colleague, who arrived within minutes (thanks to the watching women!) make photographs of the accident scene. Since no independent traffic officer came to take down particulars, these are invaluable as evidence. Very many people watched the accident happen and most are convinced it was no accident. But that was not my idea. I saw the driver, he looked quite shaken and I told him that I forgave him, which gave me great peace of mind.

Like all our many troubled victims, I also had to wait one hour for an ambulance. Why? The police had called for an ambulance for the townships, but had not stipulated that the victim was a white woman. The Edendale ambulance arrived within twenty minutes, but I was not allowed to go with it. The white ambulance could not enter the township without a police escort and that was the cause of the delay.... Martin and Gertrud went to get papers and a key from the car wreck in the afternoon. They were stopped and searched by police with cocked guns. The wreck had already been removed by 'Casper's' breakdown service!

That night I flew very gingerly to Cape Town as planned. At Groote Schuur Hospital I was re-X-rayed and they discovered that my neck injury was much more serious than had been noticed in our hospital. I had the 'hangman's fracture'. God surely had provided lots of guardian angels around me! For two weeks I lay on my back in cranial traction, my view being the ceiling, in this completely non-racial hospital. I had lots of time to think, thank and pray and also catch up on lots of crying. Especially the last few months had been rough going, emotionally.[1]

It is no wonder that most white Christians prefer not to be involved in situations like this.

Probably the most shocking and painful experience for me personally was the murder of the Anglican parish priest at St. Mark's, Imbali, Rev Victor Afrikander. I had known Victor for many years and he had been a good friend and brother priest to me. As members of the local Anglican clergy group we met together regularly, and Victor would often share his perplexity at things that were happening in the township. In recent years however, Victor seemed to have withdrawn somewhat from the rest of the clergy, chiefly I believe, because he was increasingly being overwhelmed by the demands of ministering in a parish that was in a virtual state of civil war.

On Friday, May 4th, 1990 the Pietermaritzburg clergy met, as we do on the first Friday of each month, for a service of Holy Communion in the Cathedral. This was due to be followed by our usual monthly clergy meeting. On this occasion Bishop Michael Nuttall was conducting the service. We had looked at the readings of the day, which spoke to us from the book of Romans of the way in which the Holy Spirit prays through us when we ourselves do not know how we ought to pray. Then, in a moment that I will never forget, as we knelt down to pray, the archdeacon, Victor Mkhize came in and handed a message to the Bishop. The Bishop paused for a moment and then said that he had some very shocking news to tell us. One of our number, Victor Afrikander, had been shot dead in his car in Imbali that very morning. Stunned, we continued with the service, bringing to God in prayer the awful news which we had just heard. After the service Bishop Michael said to me, 'I have had this fear for a long time, that one day it would be one of our own priests who would be killed.' We had a short meeting during which it was decided that we should all go out to Imbali. We piled into two or three cars and drove to Victor's home. The sight that awaited us was horrible. Fortunately by this time Victor's body had been removed. His car was parked outside the Rectory. The front seat was absolutely drenched in blood. Two men were trying to wash some of the blood away with a hose.

Gradually we were able to work out what had happened. Victor was driving the six-year-old daughter of a friend to school, down a shortcut which he always took on his way to town. As he stopped at the intersection a man with a brown balaclava pulled over his face walked up to the car. He reached into the car and shot Victor three times at point-blank range. He then walked away to where another man was standing. They climbed into a waiting car and drove away. We spent some time standing around the house in a state of considerable shock. I wanted to cry but I could not. Then we went into the house where Victor's widow, Constance, was sitting with some other women, friends and members of the family. We walked around the room, shaking their hands as they sat, and praying for them. Eventually we got back into our cars and went home.

The following week in the *Echo*, a local weekly newspaper which circulates mainly among black readers, Khaba Mkhize wrote:

> In any war in the history of South Africa, priests are not assassinated in broad daylight. The Reverend Victor Afrikander was a rare man of the cloth. Many ministers are scared of conducting their duties across the dangerous political divide.
>
> Who will bury us if we now kill our religious leaders here at **Less than eMadeleni**? (The abattoir). Mr Afrikander buried all and sundry without questioning their political affiliation. Prominent members of Inkatha, we are

all witnesses, he buried them in this thorny Imbali. Well-known amaQabane (comrades) have been buried by the very same shepherd we have now eliminated. In his St. Mark's parish he blessed and shepherded, you name it, members of all our political organisations.

Pietermaritzburg, search yourself: you are destroying your leaders, you are killing your women, your mothers; you are butchering your own sons – in African culture 'your child is my child'; you are creating refugees by the thousand in this place which was once King Dingane's palace and not **Less than eMadeleni**. Ask yourself, Pitymaritzburg, whose battle are you engaged in?[2]

The following Saturday Victor Afrikander's funeral took place at the Cathedral. It was jam-packed with people. Noticeably present were a large number of black youth. Frank Chikane, the General Secretary of the South African Council of Churches preached the sermon. He said, speaking of Victor, 'May we not remain in peace until we live for the ideals you lived for, the ideals of our Lord Jesus Christ. May you remain an example to us of the sacrifice of love for one's neighbour.' Frank Chikane went on, 'Because of Victor's stand for justice and peace, because of his stand for the truth, he was an embarrassment to those who kill and murder. For this reason he died. For this reason he shall ever be remembered.'

Bishop Matthew Makhaye also spoke. He told us that in these times it has become very costly to be a priest. We may be called on to pay the highest price. Many of our clergy are ministering in situations of danger and immense challenge. He concluded with a verse from 1 Corinthians 15:58: 'Therefore, my beloved brethren, be steadfast, immovable, always abounding in the work of the Lord, knowing that in the Lord your labour is not in vain.'

After the service a large group of black young people gathered on the lawns outside the Cathedral and started to sing and dance. There were large crowds milling around. Soon the youths had moved into the streets. When we finally drove away about two hundred or more young blacks were singing and dancing in the middle of Chapel Street, one of the main streets in the centre of Pietermaritzburg. Victor was a man who was known by the black youth of Imbali to be someone to whom they could turn for help. He had sought to be a true pastor to the whole of his community, and for this reason he had died. It was a privilege for me to have known him, and his death touched me deeply.

There were many other tragic and painful events that I can remember from this time. Almost daily the local newspaper *The Natal Witness* carried details of new killings, terrible murders of men, women and even children. Sometimes victims died in their burning houses, sometimes they were stabbed hundreds of times, sometimes axed to death, sometimes beheaded. Our church verger, Gilbert Ngcobo disappeared early in 1990. I had always known Gilbert as a cheerful hard-working man, with no education and certainly no political inclinations. However, one week he was clearly very upset and frightened about something. The next week he failed to arrive for work at all, which was not like him. I never saw him again. All the enquiries that we made produced no results. The local people said that they did not know what had happened to him. He may have fled to another area, in fear of his life. But one Zulu man said to me, 'I expect they killed him.' So many people were killed, so many became refugees, there was such an upheaval, that it had become very difficult to know who was alive and who was dead.

Early in 1989 something similar happened to one of our Diocesan office employees. Saimon Kunene had worked for the Diocesan offices in Durban for twenty-two years. In December 1988 he went home to his family in Ebomvini, in the Elandskop area, some miles up the valley from Sweetwaters. He never returned to work. Some months later we discovered that he had been abducted from his home and murdered. We still do not know why.

Jenny Whitley is the church secretary at the Holy Trinity Church in Hilton. In April, 1990 she wrote the following letter to *The Natal Witness*:

> I read with sadness the report in *The Natal Witness* (June 12) under the heading 'Four killed in weekend crime', where it stated 'an unknown person died ... found lying in the vicinity of Berg Street. Motive unknown.'
>
> May I please, for my own peace of mind, put the record straight. This was no 'unknown person' but a very special friend and employee. We have known Nicholas Dhladla since he was 13 and over the past 12 years he had made the most of opportunities offered,

becoming, under my husband's guidance, an expert in his field. He was a dedicated worker whose only concern was to earn a living and support his family.

At 2.15 pm on Saturday, June 9, our driver stopped in Retief Street to let off two other workers before taking Nicholas home to Sweetwaters. Nicholas was brutally dragged from the vehicle and viciously stabbed in front of a large crowd by seven assailants. His co-workers managed to get him into the back of our vehicle, whereupon he was again set upon and his throat slit.

His crime? He lived in Sweetwaters. His judges? Those who seek to impose their violent ideals on innocent victims.

May those responsible for his brutal murder rest assured that one day they will be held accountable for their despicable crime, not on this earth however because they are protected by their own lawlessness which prevents witnesses coming forward.

In the police records Nicholas has just become another statistic in the ever-spiralling violence but to us he was no 'unknown man' and his memory will remain in our hearts always.[3]

This letter expresses well the pain, bewilderment and indeed, the anger, which many people felt because of what was happening. It was difficult to know what to do. There was little that anyone could do to stop the violence, except to pray, and there was much prayer. Thankfully, things are not nearly as bad now as they were a couple of years ago.

During this time many members of our church found themselves caring for refugees from the violence. Almost everyone had someone living in their garage, or in spare rooms on their properties. Sometimes whole families came to live for a while in Hilton or Winterskloof, wherever they could find someone to take them in, just to get away from the violence in Sweetwaters and the surrounding area. Each year in the Anglican Church, one Sunday is designated a day of prayer for refugees. Before, this had been something rather distant for us, as we prayed for refugees in Mozambique or in other parts of Africa. In 1989 on Refugee Sunday, during our 9 a.m. service I said that we would have a time of open prayer for refugees who were known to us. Many people then prayed aloud by name for refugees who were living on their own properties. The problem of refugees had come home to us in Hilton.

Small groups from the church, mainly women, continued to go to Sweetwaters, day by day, throughout this time of violence. There was much prayer for protection for our people, but we felt it was vitally important not to stop the ministry at this time of testing. Sometimes it was simply too dangerous to go. On one occasion a group of women were met at the main intersection which leads into Sweetwaters. Some Zulu women had come to warn them that it was not safe and that they should turn back. Another time Jean A'Bear was driving through Sweetwaters on a Thursday morning when she noticed groups of men gathering at the roadside, armed to the teeth with sticks and assegais (spears). They were preparing for an attack on a nearby area. She kept calm, prayed hard, turned the truck round and came home fast!

The important thing was to be with those who were suffering. Simply to keep going, to be with them, to pray with them, to assist in whatever way we could. That was the main thing that we tried to do during this awful time.

CHAPTER 10
STANDING FOR THE TRUTH

> This is the judgment, that the light has come into the world, and men loved darkness rather than light, because their deeds were evil. For every one who does evil hates the light, and does not come to the light, lest his deeds should be exposed. But he who does what is true comes to the light, that it may be clearly seen that his deeds have been wrought in God. (John 3:19–21)

In South Africa the church has had a very difficult task in trying to uphold the truth as the light which drives out the darkness. There have been very strong forces which were totally committed to stopping certain aspects of the truth from being clearly and boldly upheld, and from having a wide influence. In particular, until the end of 1989, anything which might have led to a change in the white hold on political power was strongly resisted and suppressed. This led to a very serious and complex challenge for the church.

The Anglican Church in South Africa, along with many other churches has for many years opposed and resisted the system of racial discrimination and white supremacy. The Bishops and synods of the church have gone on record, time and again, in their opposition to apartheid and all that flows from it. There have been attempts to show our concern in active practical ways, such as the call for certain forms of economic pressure. These have not always been appreciated or supported by the majority of white Anglicans, but the leadership has stuck to its convictions, even though this has meant that many whites have left the Anglican Church.

But it is at the level of the local church that the challenges are often greatest. How does one enable people who have held deeply-rooted attitudes and opinions all their lives, to understand why the church is speaking out and opposing many of these ideas and attitudes? How does one enable the members of a local congregation to become involved personally in standing for the truth on these issues? We have not found this to be easy. It is a long, slow process. However, my experience has been that through consistent biblical teaching, and through exposure to preachers and speakers from different races and backgrounds, deeply-held racial and political attitudes have slowly but surely been challenged and changed. In our church preachers who are not from a white English-speaking background are regularly invited to come and speak. We also aim to set aside certain Sundays when issues of social justice will be clearly preached on and expounded. Of course, in doing this one does encounter opposition. It seems that, certainly in white South Africa, people don't mind too much if you preach about personal sin, but many do not like to hear a preacher speak about social and political sin. Yet, of course, the

Bible has an enormous amount to say on this subject. For example, in Isaiah 58:1–4, 6–8, the Lord says:

> 'Cry aloud, spare not, lift up your voice like a trumpet; declare to my people their transgression, to the house of Jacob their sins. Yet they seek me daily, and delight to know my ways, as if they were a nation that did righteousness and did not forsake the ordinance of their God; they ask of me righteous judgments, they delight to draw near to God. "Why have we fasted and, thou seest it not? Why have we humbled ourselves, and thou takest no knowledge of it?" Behold, in the day of your fast you seek your own pleasure, and oppress all your workers. Behold, you fast only to quarrel and to fight and to hit with wicked fist. Fasting like yours this day will not make your voice to be heard on high. . . .
>
> Is not this the fast that I choose: to loose the bonds of wickedness, to undo the thongs of the yoke, to let the oppressed go free, and to break every yoke? Is it not to share your bread with the hungry, and bring the homeless poor into your house; when you see the naked, to cover him, and not to hide yourself from your own flesh? Then shall your light break forth like the dawn, and your healing shall spring up speedily; your righteousness shall go before you, the glory of the Lord shall be your rear guard.'

Or what about James 5:1, 4–6:

> Come now, you rich, weep and howl for the miseries that are coming upon you....
>
> Behold, the wages of the labourers who mowed your fields, which you kept back by fraud, cry out; and the cries of the harvesters have reached the ears of the Lord of hosts. You have lived on the earth in luxury and in pleasure; you have fattened your hearts in a day of slaughter. You have condemned, you have killed the righteous man; he does not resist you.

There are many other passages that deal clearly with God's concern about social and economic justice, about the needs of the poor and the oppressed.[1] Such passages are directly relevant to modern South African society. Therefore it is vital that we grapple with them and clearly and appropriately apply them to the situation that we are in. In the course of raising these issues in the church we have found ourselves facing controversy and dissatisfaction amongst our own church members. Some have left and gone elsewhere. In fact, at one stage, it was a regular occurrence for me to receive a letter or a visit from a parishioner or a church family, informing me that they had decided to leave the Anglican Church because of the 'politics' in the church. I did not find this easy at all. It is hard for a pastor to lose members of his congregation over issues like this. During this period we also found it hard to attract new families to the church. There was a widespread resistance to the Anglican Church in general amongst non-churched white families. We were seen as the 'sanctions church', the church that was too involved in politics.

Yet we attempted to handle these difficult questions in a sensitive and consistently biblical manner. In the long term I believe that this has borne much fruit. Our congregation seems to me to be comparatively well-prepared for the changes that the 'new South Africa' is bringing. Many white people, and even white Christians, are facing the future in a dramatically changed South Africa with great anxiety and apprehension. There is still much prejudice and bitterness in the white community as a whole. Yet where the local church has taken the lead in enabling their people to understand what the Bible has to say about apartheid and social justice, there is a readiness to accept change, and a willingness to work for reconciliation and for a just society.

At one point I was particularly feeling the pain of trying to deal with the opposition of a number of church people to our stand on these issues. I told our church eldership that I thought that perhaps it was time for us to take a softer line, and for a while not to focus so much on this area, in order to help these people to stay in the church. The elders unanimously replied that we had to be true to our faith and to the Scriptures, and that we must not compromise, even if it did mean that some people would leave. This was an enormous encouragement and support to me. It showed me also, again, the great value of shared leadership in the local church. If I had tried to stand alone on some of these issues, I simply could not have coped.

So a number of preachers and leaders, both from within the church and from outside, consistently spoke about such issues as the plight of detainees, conscientious objectors and the situation in the townships. The relationship between the church and politics was a constant concern. I tried myself to address this issue regularly, in order to help people grasp what the church was trying to say. In September 1988 I wrote a letter to the whole parish in which I tried to clarify our church's stand on these very sensitive and sometimes heated issues. This is what I wrote:

> Dear brothers and sisters in Christ,
>
> Over recent months I have been aware that people of our church are increasingly concerned and disturbed about what is happening in our nation, and also perhaps at the role of the church in these issues. So this month I would like to explore some of these issues with you, especially with regard to the church's role in them.
>
> The Anglican Church seems at the present time to be in the forefront of a confrontation between the church and the government. Some church leaders are calling for sanctions and disinvestment, to the dismay and anger of many church members. Some church members have left the Anglican Church and others are threatening to do so. Other churches try to avoid mixing political issues with Christianity, and because of this they attract many people to their ranks. What are we to make of all this?
>
> Our calling as the church of the Lord Jesus Christ is to be faithful to our Lord, no matter what the cost. The gospel is, in a nutshell,

a call to all people to repent of their sins and to believe in the Lord Jesus Christ. I believe that much of our problem in South Africa arises from a failure to see that racial prejudice, or racism, is sin, and therefore must be challenged and condemned by the Christian church.

Recently there has been much controversy about the blackballing of a prospective Indian member of the Victoria Club. A letter to *The Natal Witness* argued that we have the right to choose 'in our private recreational life to associate only with whites, who speak only English'. We all have the right to choose with whom we associate, although as Christians, we should be ready to go to anyone to whom Jesus points us, and especially to the poor and the outcast. However, when we base our choice on the colour of a person's skin and not on any other criteria, then we are guilty of racism. Racism, or racial prejudice, differentiates between people on the basis of their race, instead of seeing each person as equally valuable and significant in the sight of God, regardless of their colour. Martin Luther King once said, 'I have a dream that my four little children will one day live in a nation where they will not be judged by the colour of their skin but by the content of their character.' The Bible says, 'There is neither Jew nor Greek, there is neither slave nor free, there is neither male nor female; for you are all one in Christ Jesus.' (Gal. 3:28) In Christ Jesus there is neither black nor white, for we are all one in him.

The problem in South Africa is that we have built a whole legal and political system upon racial discrimination and prejudice. In other words our present society is built upon something that is sinful. The Bible teaches that the consequences of sin are death, disaster and the judgment of God. This, then, is the reason for so much of the suffering in our beloved country.

In the Gospels Jesus spoke a number of times about 'one thing'. To Martha he said 'one thing is needful'. To the rich young man he said 'one thing you lack'. Sometimes there is one thing which God asks us to do, which for various reasons we may resist and put off. This then becomes a barrier to many other things which God is wanting to do in our lives. In our land there is one thing that needs to happen, and until we do that one thing, nothing else will solve our problems. Our government has tried many things, but until they deal with the sin of racism in the laws and structures of our society, they will not succeed in bringing peace and unity to South Africa.

It is clear from the Bible that the church has a prophetic role in the nation. When there is sin in the life of the nation the church must speak out and call for repentance. That sin may be legalized abortion, it may be bribery and corruption, it may be the sin of racism. When the church has to address the authorities on such issues, it is always a difficult, painful and costly business. It calls for great courage and wisdom.

Archbishop Luwum challenged Idi Amin and paid with his life. The church in South Africa must be faithful to the biblical standards and principles which apply to our situation. For this all church leaders need great courage and wisdom. I do not agree with calls for isolation and sanctions. But I have not suffered under the system of apartheid in the way that Desmond Tutu and millions of others have. It is important for us to understand that the cause of so much of our suffering is the sin of racial discrimination. Apartheid is not God's way for human society. His way is that we should be one, united and reconciled in Christ Jesus our Lord.

The Anglican Church in South Africa has sought to be faithful to the biblical teaching about apartheid and racial discrimination. Our witness on these issues has sometimes been weak and flawed but at least we have tried to be faithful to the biblical truth, sometimes at considerable cost. I pray that we will continue to hold together as the church of the Lord Jesus Christ, in our sorrow for what has come upon our troubled land, and in a deep and unyielding commitment to work together for justice, reconciliation and peace, in the power of the Holy Spirit.

The local church is called to pray and to work for truth and justice in the community. We, in Hilton, together with most, if not all, Christians in South Africa, prayed a great deal for our land. In every service, and in weekly prayer meetings, the situation in the country was specifically mentioned.

After the imposition of a State of Emergency in 1986, we held a special weekly Eucharist on Wednesday afternoons at 5.30 p.m. with the particular purpose of praying for South Africa. Days of prayer and fasting, called by national and Diocesan church leaders, were taken seriously by many people. The fact that today there is so much hope and so much goodwill in South Africa can, I believe, be largely attributed to the enormous commitment to prayer for this country which has been evident over many years, both within South Africa and internationally.

There also needs to be action if the church is to stand for the truth in society. This needs careful thought and prayer, because the church is not just another political pressure group. What is done in the name of Christ must flow from his character and his Spirit. The primary danger for Christians, however, is not that they will do the wrong thing in confronting injustice, it is rather that they will take the easy option and do nothing, or far too little. I would like to offer two examples of Christian action against social injustice in our own community. One was the stand made by an individual Christian; the other involved the whole parish.

Richard Shorten, as mentioned earlier, came to spend a year in the parish in 1985. In his final year of training for the ordained ministry, he was sent by the Bishop to us for a year of parish experience before he went on to be ordained. Shortly after Richard had moved into Hilton he went to the local library and enquired about becoming a member. In the course of his conversation with the librarian he asked whether blacks were allowed to

Standing for the Truth

be members of the Hilton library, and said that his conscience would not allow him to join the library if membership was restricted to whites only. The librarian didn't know the answer to this question: until this point only whites had ever been members. She said she would find out. A short while later Richard was informed that blacks would be welcome to become members of the Hilton library. A difficult issue had been raised, as a result of Richard's courage and his commitment to a non-racial South Africa. A decision had been taken and the matter was clarified, and one more small step had been made in the struggle against apartheid.

The second example was a far more serious and difficult matter. At the end of 1986 the Bishop appointed a curate, Gary Thompson, to serve at our church. We had not previously had a curate on our staff, and so we had to look for a house for Gary and his family. Fortunately at exactly this time a retired priest who was living in Hilton decided to return to parish work, and he offered his house to us. We gratefully accepted his offer.

The Bishop appoints clergy to parishes, not on the basis of race, but according to who, in his judgment, is the right person for a particular job. As Gary is a so-called 'coloured', we felt that it would be wise for us to apply for a Group Areas permit. Under the Group Areas Act it was necessary to have such a permit in order to legally live in a group area which was allocated to a race group other than one's own. These permits could take up to six months to be processed, so in the meantime Gary and his family moved into their house and he began his work in Hilton. About six weeks after the Thompsons had moved in, we discovered to our horror that one of his neighbours was organising a petition to stop Gary from living in Hilton. Many of the people in his street had already signed this petition. Soon the press got hold of this story, and it received wide publicity both locally and nationally. 'Petition in Hilton to evict coloured priest', read a large headline in one paper. 'Hilton is confronted with a Group Areas Act problem', read another.

The church wardens and elders met together and issued a statement to the press, saying, 'We believe there is a point of Christian principle involved here, and we are resolved not to be influenced by racially-based pressures to remove the Thompson family.' We also visited all those who had signed the petition, and after discussion, all of them, except the one who had organised the petition, agreed to withdraw their objections. Eventually, after some months of great tension and at times a real sense of physical danger, the necessary permit was granted. Gary and his family were able to stay, legally, in Hilton.

It was a painful and difficult experience for us. However, on reflection, I can see that much good came out of it. Our church was compelled to make a stand publicly in our own community on a matter of Christian principle. We were saying by our actions and not just our words that we do not accept the Group Areas Act and the way in which it divides our society and even divides the body of Christ. We were publicly confronting the evil of racial prejudice and discrimination.

As a result of such actions, the Group Areas Act was beginning to be questioned and broken

Standing for the Truth

down. The Church of the Ascension was the first to challenge the idea that Hilton could remain a whites-only community by publicly placing a so-called non-white family to live and minister in Hilton. This resulted in a time of much stress and tension for the leadership of our church. I know that it was by prayer more than anything else that we were able to come through that time. It is not easy to cope with threats of violence, nor is it easy to be seen to be taking a stand on a controversial issue, and by so doing making enemies in one's own community. Yet this situation was very familiar to the psalmist, and many times Gary and I found great strength and help in saying Morning Prayer together, and in reading words such as these from Psalm 56:1–4:

> Be gracious to me, O God, for men trample upon me;
> all day long foemen oppress me;
> my enemies trample upon me all day long,
> for many fight against me proudly.
> When I am afraid,
> I put my trust in thee.
> In God, whose word I praise,
> in God I trust without a fear.
> What can flesh do to me?

Indeed we were able to trust in God to defend and protect us and to bring us through. Gary did not have to move, until such time as he was appointed to take charge of a parish in his own right.

Again the words of the Psalms express our own experience, and the knowledge that we have of

God's faithfulness, care and protection: 'With God we shall do valiantly, It is He who will tread down our foes.' (Psalm 60:12)

Of course, what we experienced in this situation was but a small taste of what many black people deal with daily in South Africa. The Bible makes it clear that if we stand for the truth for the sake of Jesus Christ we will suffer persecution. Yet for many white Christians this is not at all part of their experience of being a follower of Jesus Christ, and prior to this, it had not been part of my experience either. I did not like the experience, but I have to say that through this I discovered in a new way the meaning of Christian discipleship. True discipleship means walking with Jesus in the way of the cross. Jesus said to his disciples, 'If any man would come after me, let him deny himself and take up his cross and follow me.' (Mark 8:34) The way of the cross is the way of suffering and persecution, unpopularity and self-denial. It is also the way of love. It is only through the cross that we find the reality of the resurrection life of Jesus. It is by sharing the sufferings of Jesus that we also share his victory and his glory.

* * *

In Ephesians 6:12–13, Paul tells us:

> For we are not contending against flesh and blood, but against principalities, against the powers, against the world rulers of this present darkness, against the spiritual hosts of wickedness in the heavenly places. Therefore take the whole armour of God, that you may

be able to withstand in the evil day, and having done all, to stand.

In verse 18, he says: 'Pray at all times in the Spirit, with all prayer and supplication. To that end keep alert with all perseverance, making supplication for all the saints.' It is important to recognize that we are involved in a spiritual battle, both in our own personal discipleship and in confronting the powers of evil in society.

We are not primarily involved in a struggle against 'flesh and blood', political organizations or individual people. It is against 'powers and principalities', spiritual forces of evil, which control both individual people and whole communities, that we are contending. The violence in Sweetwaters clearly demonstrated the evil spiritual forces that were at work in that situation. People were not simply being murdered – they were being killed in the most gruesome manner, often stabbed or hacked over and over again. What could cause people to commit such terrible deeds? Only a very powerful force of evil, which had taken control of the hearts of people.

It is particularly through prayer, with fasting, that we can overcome these powers and principalities, as St. Paul makes clear in Ephesians 6:14. We have experienced the effectiveness of such prayer with fasting, particularly I believe in leading to many of the changes which have now taken place in South Africa. I am certain that it is because of the prayers of many many people that, in spite of all that has taken place in this land, there is today great hope for a new, just and peaceful South Africa. But prayer and action must go together. Prayer must be part of an obedient Christ-like life, which will expose evil and drive it out, as light drives out darkness. This will always be costly, for it will mean being involved personally in the battle between good and evil.

This was brought home forcibly to me and to many people in our church by our experience over Gary's house. We are involved in a war, a battle against the powers and principalities, the spiritual hosts of wickedness in the heavenly places. That battle can only be won by putting on the whole armour of God, by upholding truth, righteousness and justice, by proclaiming the gospel of peace and salvation in Jesus Christ, by faith and prayer and the Word of God. Above all in that battle we must hold fast to the cross of Christ, for that is where he defeated the power of sin and death and evil, once and for all, and then rose victorious on the third day.

CHAPTER 11
THE LOCAL CHURCH IN ACTION

Much of this book thus far has been my own story and struggles. However, I am just one member of the Church of the Ascension and my story does not by any means reflect the experience of the whole parish. In this chapter I would like to share some of the insights and experiences of other members of the parish who have been involved in the Sweetwaters ministry.

Sarah Dottridge goes to Sweetwaters every Monday morning in the parish truck. This vehicle is a necessity for this work because of the many rough tracks and steep inclines which have to be covered. When there has been rain, many of these become impassable for any vehicle except a four-wheel drive. Sarah and Pat Caldwell started this work in 1985, and it has continued to develop and flourish since then.

Pat Caldwell now works full-time at a local agricultural college, and so she now organises the ordering of materials, the book-keeping and marketing of the blankets which the women make. Sarah Dottridge, together with a small band of women from our church, plus the occasional visitors, drives down to Inadi on most

Monday mornings of the year. They first pay a short visit to the Mbanjwa Primary School where 400 children are fed daily with a cup of hot soup. A woman named Detrina is employed to run the feeding scheme, with back-up support from our church. Sarah and her group then drive a short distance to a small church where the blanket-making co-operative is based. Wool is given out, blankets are received, and sundry other needs and questions are attended to. This is followed by a meeting in the church itself, usually attended by forty or fifty women, a few men and quite a lot of small children. There is a time for singing, sharing of news, teaching from the Bible and prayer for particular needs.

I asked Sarah why she has continued to be committed to this work after quite a few years now. She replied:

> Well, I feel that I can do something here. I can make the world just a little bit different. Maybe it sounds a bit presumptuous, but I can be of some use by doing this. There is an obvious crying need here, and, especially as a Christian, I would hope that I can make a contribution towards making this country a better place. And I believe that God has called me to do this work; if I didn't believe that, I wouldn't do it.

I then asked Sarah about some aspects of her work, which I had observed during a recent trip to Sweetwaters with her group.

Ian On the way to the school we stopped to

The Local Church in Action

pick up a man named Bonginkosi, who is not able to use his legs at all. He was lifted into the truck and spent the whole morning with us. Tell me more about him.

Sarah Bonginkosi is a paraplegic who lives there, next to the road, with his mother and his step-father, who have no work. He has no pension, although we have been trying to organise one for him, but he doesn't actually have it yet, so he's in fact destitute. We've tried to get him to do blankets, but he's left-handed and he cannot crochet. So we do give him a little remuneration for helping us. He is always so wonderfully cheerful, and he's quite a force in his own way. If someone comes along who is drunk, he's the first to say, 'That man must be spoken to about his behaviour.' He came because we used to meet at old Richard Nkomo's house. Someone used to carry him down there. Errol Hoole made him a little wooden cart and then he got a wheelchair. Now we take him in the truck. He had nowhere to ride in his wheelchair because it is too rough. He's a quiet man, but very clear in his spiritual walk. He knows where he stands and despite his physical disability, he is a force in the community.

Ian At the school there is a classroom with 150 children in the class, the floor is badly broken up, and the children used to simply kneel on plastic bags, because there were no benches or desks. But you were able to do something about this.

Sarah   Yes, this was in the middle of winter — it was ghastly. Save the Children Fund provided benches, teacher's tables and chairs. The teachers didn't even have tables. The desks were too expensive, and we could only get a few. I went for the option of more, for more children.

Ian   And you organised toilets for the school.

Sarah   That was an answer to prayer! We prayed for so long. They were all using a hole with rusting corrugated iron around it, and two very dicey concrete slabs over the hole which they squatted on. The stench was indescribable. What made it worse was that the hole was above the fresh water spring which is the source of water for the whole area. It has contaminated all the water, so they cannot use that water any more. Save the Children Fund gave us some money but we were able to get the loos (latrines) at an incredibly cheap price — it was a miracle. We now have fifteen loos for boys, and girls, and teachers. Before, even the teachers had to use that terrible hole. It's made a huge difference to stopping disease, because the new loos have chimneys and doors and everything. The school committee paid for the holes to be dug, and the older school children and the teachers assembled them, so it was their project as well. The whole area wants these loos now — I keep getting phone calls at home, from people in Edendale and all over.

The Local Church in Action

Ian And now you're trying to get water at the school.

Sarah There will be no piped water in this area in the near future — possibly in 1995 piped water will be put in. So we have got a couple of rainwater tanks. We need to bury them, or at least one of them, so that the water is available for the children, and not used by the householders in the surrounding area. So we'll have a portable hand pump, so that they can take it in at night. It has to be a hand pump, because there's no electricity, and they'll never get that, as far as I can see.

Ian The feeding scheme seems to be running well.

Sarah Yes, although there is another whole train of thought, which says that they should be running it themselves. They should be raising the money from the children, and getting the soup, and paying Detrina. But our thought is that this place is so poor that you're not going to get the very poorest doing that, and we want to feed the poorest. We don't want to feed the ones who can afford it anyway.

Ian Recently you were asked to go and pray in the home of Anna Mkhize when her husband died.

Sarah Yes, her husband died of asthma.

What it indicates is that we do go as fellow brothers and sisters in the Lord, to pray through their natural disasters, and thank goodness this was a natural one and not political. What was not natural was that they couldn't get him to hospital. My heart just bled for them. It was a privilege for us that we were seen as brothers and sisters, that they wanted us to come and pray. Anna is a very bold member of that body; she's been in the group for ages, a lovely woman.

Ian   And what about Salome?

Sarah   Well Salome came up to Pat and said, 'Why don't you use the church?' She's the caretaker of the church and has the keys to it. It's a Lutheran church, although I don't know who the minister is, or if there is one. There may be one who comes up every couple of months. But Salome is a very dedicated woman; and very motivated. She started a crêche, which we've helped, but *not* taken over. We sent her to T.R.E.E. (Training and Resources in Early Education) to be trained, for instance. Salome is a very spiritual woman too, and as you know, a wonderful translator. With her you can say what you want to say without having to keep simplifying, and its hard to express yourself sometimes in very basic language. Ever since we've been down there she's been our translator.

Ian   And Lafina?

The Local Church in Action

Sarah   She has so many children, eight at least; plenty, plenty children. And she also is such a lovely person. She used to look after a man who died, who was terribly crippled. She was next-door neighbour to him, and she cared for him and fed him and clothed him. She now does blankets to keep going. I don't know what her husband does, or what the situation is, but she has very meagre income. One problem which we've skirted, which we've never really gone into, which I know Dave A'Bear does, is the whole problem of husbands and boyfriends and the morals of all that.

Ian   She fed and clothed the dying man?

Sarah   Yes, and when we heard this, we were able to help and to supplement. When we hear of needs, we can do this. But if you don't go down, how will you ever know the needs? That's why I say that you've got to go into the area. How else will you ever know? The whole world has needs but you can only deal with that which comes to your particular sphere of knowledge, and so often the need won't be met because there are people no-one knows about. That's why I think you've got to *GO*. And I personally feel you've got to go once a week. There are an average of forty to fifty people there each week. How can we even know what's going on if we don't go once a week? I also feel its got to be a commitment. For me, nothing comes before

Sweetwaters on Monday. I actually see it as my job. People ask do I work? I say 'No', but actually I see this as my job. There has to be a commitment with something like this. When we first went, the people said, 'Oh, we had somebody before doing soup.' When we got there we saw one of those three legged pots. I said, 'Where did that come from?' 'Oh,' they said, 'the people before, but they stopped.' Each year for the first few years I remember the almost-amazement when we came back after the Christmas holidays, that we were the same people who kept coming every week. It's a trust thing, isn't it. It's a thing that I'm prepared to give this time, to give this slice of my life. But only God will give you that ability to stick at it. That's why I don't think doing something for charity will work. It wouldn't work for me, put it that way. Only when God institutes it, do people have the right motivation for going, and the ability to stick at it. In our age group, in this generation particularly, people seem to start things and then so often seem to give it up. Unless the Holy Spirit initiates and gives us the ability to keep going . . .

Ian   Tell us about Beauty.

Sarah   She's the one who sells apples on Monday mornings to make a bit of extra income. And she does her blankets, so she's sitting there making her blanket and selling her apples. It's nothing to do with us; she did that on her own completely. Her husband has become like a two-year-old child. I don't know whether it's a stroke or what it is. She's a wonderful person. And now she's bringing those two old ladies, her mother and her aunt. They've only been coming this year; before it was just Beauty. And she walks all that way with the apples on her head. Occasionally we pick her up, but she's always there. We always give her a lift back. I tell you, its very humbling. I come back and I have very different priorities. I mean, the poor will be with you always, and I'm not saying we've all got to become poor, but in this country I think that people are the poorer themselves for not knowing how others live. You can't just live in your own little world. You are the one who is poor, poor in spirit.

Ian   How are we enriched by the poor? Could you give me an example of this?

Sarah   Well, there was a woman who came to us and she had broken her arm, and when she took it out of plaster, I don't know what went wrong, but it went sick and weak. We prayed for her arm, and brought her a squash ball so that she could exercise it, and it came right. So then, she learnt how to do blankets. And as a sort of thanksgiving she said, 'I want to give you something; you give us a lot.' She has brought us a whole lot of pumpkins and mealies for the last three weeks, because she said, 'It's time for harvesting, I want to share.' I think that its wonderful that she could do that for us. That's the sort of sisterhood, that's loving one another, isn't it? It's a real kind of community.

Ian   Is there anything else you would like to share with us?

Sarah   I do think that it's wonderful that the church supports this. We do definitely feel that this is a church thing. You need the authority of the church. I always say that we come from the church in Hilton. So it is the church in Hilton which is wanting to reach into Sweetwaters, and I think you need that authority behind you, besides the support, the prayer and the financial support, but you need the authority. I really believe that.

* * *

Much of the Sweetwaters ministry of our church has been made possible by the pioneering work of Graham Beggs. Graham was appointed in January, 1980 as a full-time parish worker to develop this ministry. He was recognised by the church as someone who had particular gifts in working with the poor. Graham also had much experience in the field of rural development, and in working with the Zulu people in various development projects.

Some years earlier when he had been working for the Methodist Mission in Zululand, a visiting professor from the USA had recognised that Graham had a unique gift in developing credible relationships with the poor. As a result Graham

The Local Church in Action

and his family were invited to the USA so that Graham could undertake a one-year study programme in rural development. Two years after he returned from the United States Graham was invited by the Church of the Ascension Council to come and work as a parish worker in Sweetwaters. The Parish Council were looking for someone to go into Sweetwaters and make an impact, to bring in running water and roads and that kind of thing. But at this point the church leadership also said to Graham, 'We are setting you apart as a man of God to listen.' So Graham began to move amongst the poor, feeling that he had been thrust into something that was beyond his abilities. There was at this time quite a lot of confusion in the church about Graham's role and many did not fully understand what he was attempting to do. The consequence of this was a certain amount of turmoil. I asked Graham about this, and about some of the difficulties and tensions of those earlier years of the Sweetwaters ministry.

Graham   What I think I was learning is that what God gives for us to do by obedience is intensely personal. What I was aware of in myself was a depth of relationship with the Father through the Son. And for me obedience was out of the confidence of that relationship, to be just where God had asked me to be. But part of the frustration was that I was also beginning to come to grips with the conventions of man which so easily direct what is acceptable and what is not acceptable, what is pleasing and what is not pleasing. I had to take a leap of faith, to simply obey God, which made it very difficult to interpret that to other people.

Ian Was there a lack of understanding of the costly obedience that you were speaking about?

Graham What God was speaking about was not just Sweetwaters but about Africa. The beginning of the way was through Sweetwaters. I think people understood that, and that was what they found threatening, not going to Sweetwaters, but taking the first step and knowing that there was something else. I think also that part of the frustration was that many prophecies had been affirmed over me, not just through the local body, but through people beyond as well. I knew that these were true, but I couldn't grasp them, even in my own life.

Ian So often prophecy is like that because it is something that is in the future and beyond our experience. That's what it was like for Abraham. It is something that one has to grasp by faith, without understanding intellectually what is involved.

Graham A previous step in my life was in 1967, '68 and '69 when I worked for the Methodist Mission. All that I had to offer were my hands in those days, but in that offering the Lord blessed me with his grace to the extent that people saw something different, and something different was happening in peoples' lives that I wasn't even vaguely aware of. It was when a visiting professor from the States asked, 'Who taught you these things?', and I answered him, 'What are you talking about?', that he said, 'The way you go about this.' He was talking about community development strategies and social work philosophies, and how one actually reaches people, how one develops a credible relationship with the poor.

Ian But when you started work with the Church of the Ascension there was this misunderstanding of your role, which must have been frustrating for you.

Graham The mandate that was given from this church was to hear what God was saying. This was something quite unique, because I then got amongst the poor and it was frightening, because I know what it is like to be thrust into something which is way beyond your range. The consequence of that has been the turmoil, because God did speak, and God did give direction. But it touched people in places where it hurt and the very simple word that God was speaking was, 'Repent'. But people said, 'What do you mean, "Repent?" We've repented. We are Christian believers. We are born again.' But what the Lord was speaking about was a whole list of presumptuous sins which we are only going to discover when we obey his command. This was another secret which the Lord unleashed for me – that when you obey the Word, that is when you become aware of your sin. So the Lord humbled me. He said, 'Don't think that you are equipped for this. You're not. But it is as you go there, you are going to become equipped, because you will first be confronted with righteousness, you will repent, and then the equipping comes.' At that time I could not articulate all this. I couldn't understand the frustration, I couldn't put it into words but I was aware of it happening. But now, because of God's faithfulness I'm able to help other people in going through this and I'm able to channel them.

Ian What would you say about the way that God has now worked, through what was initiated in those years?

Graham Well, we've seen a lot. I think we still see confusion. There are still people who are looking at the people as they are. But there are people certainly who have had a revelation of God's glory, and of the darkness of mens' lives in Sweetwaters. The desire of my heart has been in prayer to seek that the people to whom I ministered would have a revelation of the glory of Jesus Christ, and that has been a constant prayer of mine, that the people would have conviction by the Holy Spirit of righteousness and of sin and of judgment, because that is what it says in John Chapter 16. You can preach the gospel, you can minister to people, you can help widows, you can bury the dead, but unless people as a result of your ministry have a deep conviction of righteousness, by the Holy Spirit, there is no fruit. Jesus said that there would be no fruit unless we are abiding in him. I have seen in many people a growing awareness of the Lord's purposes for eternal fruit to be borne out of our going in obedience. I can say that because I have also seen a lot of people go and they want to give it up, or they say, 'What are we getting out of this?', or 'What can we see for it?'

If you want to evaluate it on a worldly basis, there is nothing to show for it. At our Parish vestry meeting, what is there really to show for what happens in Sweetwaters? Perhaps Jean comes back with a testimony, or Sarah comes back with a testimony. What the Lord is saying about Sweetwaters is that it is one step out, then another step out, then another step out, because he wants us, in terms of the Great Commission, to make disciples of all peoples. I believe the Lord nurtures us amongst our own people. But unless there is a dependence upon God, faith doesn't operate in our lives. I think we've seen a lot of this in people like Roger and Colleen for example. They know that being there, not doing anything but being there, God is at work. It's spirituality isn't it. It is a degree of spirituality.

Ian   What is a credible relationship with the poor, from a Christian point of view?

Graham   It's all to do with power and influence. A poor person is a person who has no choices and no alternatives. He's obliged to live just as he is. And so a poor person is subject to anybody who is over him, whether it is a bus driver, or a school teacher, a nurse or anyone. The poor capitulate, because of their bondage in poverty, and out of fear of losing what they've got. What the Lord taught me was when we were building a church in Zululand. It was winter, and it was a drought, and the water just dripped out of the spring. In my quiet time that morning, I'd been talking to the Lord, and looking at these foundations and thinking about how much concrete we had to mix, how hot it was, and how nice it would be to get home on Friday, and to be all finished. The Lord said to me, very clearly, 'Go to the spring and only draw water when there is nobody from the community there.' I had these two drums that I had to fill before we could do anything. I went off to get the water thinking that in an hour or so I would be back, and I was there all day. As women came I had to retreat so that they could take their water. The Lord was saying to me, 'This is not your water; this is not your community, this is not your spring, that is not your church; this is not your strength. I brought you here, I'm organising this. Just do it my way.' At the end of the day when finally I had my eighty-eight gallons of water, I was driving back and I met many of the people on the way just resting under the trees. The Lord touched me with a grace that brought me to understand that in the Lord Jesus Christ we can be poor to the poor but we are enriched in Christ, and in your poverty to the poor they are enriched in Christ.

Ian   What do you mean being poor to the poor?

Graham   It means laying down everything. In other words, the influences that I might have had, being without the power that I might have had, having been there under authority to build a church. All of those things, to lay them down, that there is nothing, nothing in me to say to a poor person, 'Will you wait? This is important. I need to draw. This comes first'. So the Lord taught me that, in order to develop such a credible relationship, one has to be received by the poor and lifted up by them, to where they are. Now this is the principle that I've used, because I'm aware of it. It is a foundation principle. So when at Zamma Zamma (in Northern Zululand) we go out in ministry, this is part of the waiting that takes place. It's what is involved, when I go to Zamma Zamma, in riding the bicycle or in walking. You're in a position where the poor are able to say, 'May I help you?' If they find you and they don't look at you then as a strong man, then this is something which is not because of who we are – it is Christ. You can forsake all things, and then he will do something and as those people offer you food or a place to sleep or water to drink there is a bond. Jesus says, 'Whoever gives to one of these little ones even a cup of cold water because he is a disciple, truly, I say to you, he shall not lose his reward.' (Matt. 10.42)

There is a principle at stake here. The poor have got absolutely nothing material to give, but if there is one way that they can share themselves it is to say, 'Can I help you?' That's the only way the poor can do it and this is something that is very difficult to share with people or even to teach. But I have discovered that if the relationships are interpersonal, and the poor have a trust in you, because there is no perceived threat of being trampled, then you haven't got to promise them anything, and that is the liberty of Christ. You haven't got to say, 'I'll build your house,' or 'I'll fix that', or 'I'll do this', because the relationship is in Jesus. It's the servanthood of Jesus. That is in essence what is contained here. The same is true of ministry to the dying and the sick. You can't go there strong. You've got to go so that even the dying person says, 'Just sit with me'. He asks you to be there. Once you're there, there is power in the prayer because Jesus is present. 'Where two or three come together in my name, there am I with them.' But as long as the self is there, or you're dependent on self, yes, the Lord is there, but he can't do quite as much.

Ian In your first few years in Sweetwaters I think this was part of the puzzlement because this is what you were doing. You were not putting in piped water or sanitation, you were just going in and listening and praying and being there, and gradually, slowly building those relationships of trust.

Graham And one can say that it has paid off, to God's glory. I don't go in there daily now, but I still get requests from the chief or other people who say, 'Please come'. The relationship is there – it is cemented. In fact, one of the things I have had to do is try and wean myself off some of the dependencies of some of these relationships. All kinds of people come to ask for help, to use the telephone, and so on. What I've learned is the authority in Christ to speak into their lives and to discern when they really are seeking something, and when they are just hoodwinking. In the Spirit we do have the authority to admonish and to see people's lives being turned. For me that has been one of the greatest blessings, in being set free from the fear of offending a poor person, to have the liberty in Christ, to know that his word is going to set that poor person free from a bondage. And sometimes it has to be a strong word. But that is what comes for me from that obedience, and out of that, submission to the poor as the servant of servants.

Ian What do you think the Lord is wanting to do now in the church, especially in the Church of the Ascension?

Graham I don't believe that things have changed. I believe that in all our work in Sweetwaters we need to keep as the bottom line that we go out of obedience. We go ill-equipped, but we go in faith. We must expect a crisis. We must anticipate a personal crisis, of being out of our depth. If you speak to any of the people who have been to Sweetwaters, they will say, 'On this day I just didn't know what was going to happen.' That is where repentance comes. If we seek reconciliation in the Lord Jesus Christ, reconciliation is the fruit of repentance. You cannot have reconciliation where people are not freed by the grace of the Lord Jesus to be nothing. You might have two extremes but you both have to become nothing to be reconciled in Christ.

I believe that in our nation, where we obey in a particular situation or event, there is a major breakthrough in the heavenly realms. This is the spiritual warfare which flows out of obedience. If the Lord says we are to do this in Sweetwaters, that is a specific location; you can't do it anywhere else, and we can't be anywhere else, because we are limited to where our bodies can be. But if we obey I do know that Christ is able to do something far greater.

Obedience brings a wonderful blessing. One of the deepest prayers in my heart is that we at the Church of the Ascension might enter into God's grace through that obedience, to taste the blessing that he has. And I tell you, it is a wonderful, wonderful blessing to be among a strange people, with a strange language, under the authority of Jesus, and to see people set free. You just see God working, and you're aware that for everything you've

The Local Church in Action

seen on the ground, its been multiplied in the heavenlies. For me, intercession and spiritual warfare cannot be done in an armchair. You've got to stand in the place, with your soles on the ground, because obedience is necessary. Jesus could have stayed in heaven and prayed all those prayers. But obedience was the first step, and everything else is built onto that.

CHAPTER 12
LEARNING OBEDIENCE

For Graham Beggs, obedience is the starting point in Christian discipleship. As we go out in costly obedience to the Lord Jesus Christ, we are plunged into a crisis of dependence upon God. Many members of our church have discovered that for themselves as they have obeyed God's call to go to Sweetwaters, to Zululand, and, more recently, to Mozambique. Dave and Jean A'Bear had known Graham Beggs for many years, long before he came to the Church of the Ascension. They have been closely involved with him, and have for many years formed part of a small group which has met weekly to pray for, and to support Graham and his work. In recent years Dave and Jean have themselves opened up new areas of ministry in Sweetwaters.

Dave goes every Saturday morning at 7 a.m. to a house belonging to a woman named Dora, who has worked for the A'Bears for a number of years now. There he meets with a group of Zulu men and women, and leads a time of teaching from the Bible and prayer for various needs. His chief concern has been to reach Zulu men who work in Pietermaritzburg during the week. This has proved to be a slow and difficult task, but a number

Learning Obedience

of men have been drawn into this group and have come to faith in Christ.

Jean leads a similar ministry to women and children which is based at the old St. Michael's Church, on the boundary between Sweetwaters and Winterskloof. Many people, sometimes in desperate need, come to St. Michael's on a Thursday morning looking for help and for prayer. Once a month a service of Holy Communion is held in Zulu. This church has become a meeting point between black and white, a place of prayer and worship where all are welcome and where the needs and cries of the poor can be heard, and brought in prayer to God.

I asked Dave and Jean what had enabled them to persevere in the work in Sweetwaters over many years now.

Dave I think that the first thing that I've learned from the work there is that, because God gave our church a direction to go there, he has blessed and anointed our going. He has led us to relate to particular people that he has prepared for us to meet. Those kinds of meetings and relationships have been very important and strategic in enabling us to continue. I think also that what one learns is that as you step out onto the water – and it is like stepping out on water, because you don't know how deep it is – you discover that because it is by obedience, and therefore by faith, the Lord is there, and he does uphold you. I think often that when I go on a Saturday, I feel very much that this is the last thing that I want to do. But when you get there, you actually feel the empowering of the Lord to be there and to do this.

Jean The main thing that I have learnt from going is summarized by this verse from Isaiah 50:10:

> Who among you fears the Lord
>   and obeys the voice of his servant,
> who walks in darkness
>   and has no light,
> yet trusts in the name of the Lord
>   and relies upon his God?

There are many times when you know that you are walking in darkness, and you cannot see any light. You have to rely absolutely upon God, for example when you are praying for people in desperate situations, such as people who have no food. The easiest thing is to take food. But to pray for a person who has no food, and to believe that God is going to provide for that person, that is to be, as it were, in the darkness where you cannot see the light.

Ian Why is that somehow more difficult in Sweetwaters than it is, say, in the Church of the Ascension.

Dave One reason is that you're out of your context culturally and you're out of your context language-wise. You're also in a situation

Learning Obedience

where the material need is much more obvious than the spiritual need. So there is a pressure to try and meet the material need and ignore the spiritual need.

Jean   But also in meeting the spiritual needs of people, you have to rely absolutely on the Lord, because you are dealing at the spirit level, and you are dealing with sin. I know that is true in our church as well, that we are dealing with the spiritual problems of people. But the African people are very spiritual people and many of them are demonised through their spiritual beliefs, and many of their physical problems come from spiritism.

Ian   In our own church we can rely on giving people advice or counselling or whatever, but in Sweetwaters there is less ability to rely on things like this.

Jean   The original word that the Lord gave us through Graham in 1980 was, 'Wait on the Lord, and go in faith.' That was the essence of what God was saying. Going in faith is very different from going by sight. If we go in our own strength, in our own ways of sorting things out for people, we are not going to have the testimony that comes from going by faith.

Ian   But the testimony of going by faith is a strange thing. It is not just so many healings, so many conversions, and so on. It is often a much more mysterious thing.

Dave   For me the testimony of faith is obedience and whether it's obedience to a call to preach, or just to be somewhere, or to read a book, or to pray, whatever it is, it's simply obedience. It means that you believe that God has got a plan, even if it seems a ridiculous thing that you are being asked to go and do.

Jean   In Romans it says that no-one who puts their trust in the Lord will be ashamed. Our senses want knowledge of what is happening; we want to know that God has heard our prayers, we want to see the results, we want to hear from people what has happened. And so there is a testing of faith. But maybe in three months time we will see; or maybe we'll never see. But I feel the Lord does reward us, at times when we need encouragement. For example, there is old Mrs Hlongwane. After her husband died she turned to drink and everyone gave up on her. Then her children arrived one day at St. Michael's. They were destitute and crying. The Lord said to me, 'I was in prison and you visited me.' He's been telling me for over a year to get out of St. Michael's and into the homes of the people. But I had held back. So now Nan Hopkins and I went out to her home and we anointed her with oil and prayed for her, and there is a testimony there. Nan could not believe her eyes when she saw how that woman had been healed.

Learning Obedience

So God does reward us, just when we need some encouragement, but we can't depend on always having our senses satisfied.

Ian   Yes, I have come to see that the Sweetwaters work is really, for us, a challenge to obedience.

Dave   For me the Sweetwaters work is really just a step on a walk, because from there God is going to lead people on into all sorts of different things.

Ian   How did you first become involved in the Sweetwaters work?

Dave   Well, I had known Graham long before he came to Hilton. I was able to understand something of what he was saying to the church, and I started to go regularly with him to Sweetwaters. I had grown up on a farm, and I was accustomed to Zulu people, and I could speak some Zulu, so I slotted in more easily, perhaps, than some people in the church. For about four or five years we used to have a Tuesday morning prayer and praise meeting at 6 a.m. at St. Michael's. During that time a lot of the vision for the Sweetwaters work, and beyond, began to be formed. Then I got involved with sometimes preaching at St. Michael's, when we had a service there on Sunday nights. Then five years ago the Lord spoke to me from Exodus, Chapter 23:20 ff., which was a word from the

Lord saying to me, 'I am with you; now go. And if you go you will see me being with you'. So I started to go every week to Dora's house and, yes, God has been with me.

Ian And what about you Jean? Why have you become involved in this?

Jean Well I was one of those who didn't hear the Lord through Graham in the initial stages. I reacted to his message and to him and everything. I took quite a while to be weaned into the work. But we'd been in house groups, and had a house group in our home for years, and been involved in a lot of Christian leadership, and I was feeling very dry. And then one day I sat at my desk and read this from Matthew 28:18–19 'All authority in heaven and on earth has been given to me. Go therefore and make disciples of all nations.' And I said to myself, the Lord has said this, so I must do it. And from then it was in the going, with the gospel, and in faith that I got my food. Jesus said 'My food is to do the will of God.' So I understood that you can't just sit in groups, looking inward, in order to be fed. Your main feeding is to do the will of God, and I'm sure he wants us to be involved in an outward work. So I started going then to St. Michael's, and Graham used to go as well. But after a while he stopped going, and for a few years I went on my own every Thursday. Recently Nan has been coming with me, and it has been such a blessing to have her with me.

Learning Obedience

Ian   What is the purpose of your going to St. Michael's on Thursdays?

Jean   In Luke 4:18–19, Jesus says,
'The Spirit of the Lord is upon me,
because he has anointed me to preach good news to the poor.
He has sent me to proclaim release to the captives
and recovering of sight to the blind,
to set at liberty those who are oppressed,
to proclaim the acceptable year of the Lord.'

So the purpose is to go and to make disciples, and to bring deliverance, and to bring people into faith in Christ. At one of our Sweetwaters leaders' meetings everyone had something to report that was measurable, and one person was challenging someone else about whether their project was truly self-help. And the Lord showed me clearly that I am involved in self-help, and that is teaching the poor to live by faith. If someone can live by faith, if they know that they have a relationship with Jesus and can trust him then he will provide.

Ian   That could sound very pious and condescending, especially coming from a white person, talking about teaching the poor to live by faith.

Jean   Well, this is what God has called me to do. I accept that God has called others to do other things, like the blankets and the candles and so on. And also, what we do is not without practical help.

Dave What is often described as self-help is not actually self-help, because as long as people are there orchestrating, assisting, providing the market, or bringing the money in, or whatever it is, it is not truly self-help. What I have seen in Mozambique showed me that so many of the things which we tout as self-help fall apart when the chips are down. In fact, the only thing that will enable projects to be 'self-help' is when peoples' hearts are sufficiently transformed and in tune with Christ that they are able to live by faith, and to seek him first, and his righteousness, and then he will add all those things, and others, to them.

Ian So you are starting at the level of the heart, with the spiritual needs of people. But also, you both have a real concern for those people, and there is a depth of relationship between yourselves and them.

Jean We are all challenged by that, because we realise that it is actually going into the peoples' homes that brings the deepest relationships. I don't think that many of them would ever imagine that we would come to visit them, off the beaten track, down the bumpy road, into the hovel. And when we come there, it means an enormous amount to them. It speaks far louder than any preaching.

Learning Obedience

Dave   In the homes that I go to in the Madwaleni area, there is alcoholism, there is prostitution and all sorts of immorality, there is drug addiction, there is lots of unemployment. One could talk about development to those people, and some of them will go along with it. But there is no freedom to actually take the initiative themselves. They are not free to actually run with it. People are bound, they are not free, and the root of that is not material poverty, but spiritual poverty and spiritual bondage. People are not free because they do not have Christ in their hearts. The social conditions contribute to the problems but I don't believe that they are causative. Between the United States and Sweetwaters, you get a spectrum of crime, from highly sophisticated fraud through to murder. It just depends upon where people are intellectually, culturally, educationally, and so on, as to which route sin will take and how it will manifest itself.

Ian   What have you learnt from the people in Sweetwaters?

Dave   I am incredibly struck by the longsuffering of the poor. I don't have enough experience to know whether that is a characteristic of poverty, or whether it is a characteristic of the Zulu people, or African tribal people, particularly. The poor have so little control and so there is a longsuffering attached to being poor. In our western culture, if we have to wait for something, that absorbs a lot of energy. We sit on tenterhooks, waiting for something. But in Africa, people don't wait, they 'be'. If something is meant to happen, and it happens three hours later, it doesn't bother them in the slightest.

Jean I don't think I have learnt very much from the poor as such, because I've seen that the poor can be as bitter and resentful as anyone else. But what I have learnt is from the Christian poor, from those who are true believers in Christ and who live by faith. They are the ones who challenge my faith enormously, because of the way in which they turn in faith to Jesus in their suffering in a way that I could never identify with. And you can tell who are the true believers, because they have a testimony of a living, dynamic relationship with Jesus, who is practical. There is an old woman in her nineties, who told us she was born in the Bambata rebellion. She had a vision the other night of a hen that came into her kraal area. She shooed it off but it just wouldn't go away, and it went and sat in a tree. She told her children, 'This dream which I have had means that God is going to provide for us.' The next day she came to our service. Graham had been trying to get a chicken to her for five weeks, as a Christmas present. He had given it to me that day, and this old woman came to church and there was this live chicken there for her. She went around praising the Lord, and she said, 'Can you imagine what the children will say

Learning Obedience

when I come home with this chicken!' Now people like that really humble one.

* * *

The long-term involvement in Sweetwaters of people from our church has been, quite specifically, the result of obedience to a call from God. This call has been experienced in differing ways, and has led to differing forms of involvement. But for each person there has been this obedience in faith. Such obedience is costly, because it is long-term and requires perseverance and discipline. But because it is a response to the Lord's call those who go out in obedience find that the Lord equips and sustains them for this work. Our experience has been that as we go out God blesses us and teaches us so much, so that we are the ones who are enriched as much as anyone else.

Nicky Ing and Joan Hoole are two women who have been members of the Church of the Ascension for many years, and have built a long-standing relationship with a group of women who meet at St. Raphael's Church in Sweetwaters. I asked Nicky Ing what led her to first become involved with the St. Raphael's group.

Nicky When I look back, I think it was because I had been with Betty Bradford to Nxamalala, much further into Sweetwaters, and she had said to me, 'If this is a ministry that you feel you would like to be involved in, there are so many other areas that could be opened up.' At that stage I didn't have access to a church vehicle, because the truck was being used on the particular day that I was free to go, so we decided that St. Raphael's would be a good place to start from, because it is close to the main road. We already knew some of the people from St. Raphael's, so we spoke to them and asked if they would like to have a Bible study. They came back to us about three weeks later and said they had discussed it and felt that this would be a good idea. We had put the initiative into their hands, we didn't mean to force our way in if it wasn't something that they themselves wanted. So we started by going every week. We used to take notes from the sermons at Hilton on Sunday, because we knew that, being Anglicans, they would have the same lectionary and the same readings for each Sunday that we had. So we went down on Tuesdays, when the Sunday readings were still fresh in their minds so we could share some thoughts on these. And inevitably we found that they also were willing to share from their side things that they had heard and they had learned. It's been very much a sharing experience. It hasn't been a going in and giving them something that we think they haven't got. It isn't like that, and never has been. We felt very humbled to see that they could offer us so much in terms of faith and joy and praise under all circumstances. They seemed to be so much more in touch with God, in a very real way, than many of the white people that we know in Hilton who have never really had to battle and struggle as they have.

Learning Obedience

Ian And you then got involved in practical ways in peoples' lives, didn't you?

Nicky Well inevitably one gets involved when in a Bible study or fellowship group of any kind, whether it is across racial barriers, or across any kind of barrier. One becomes involved with the people and their lives. So we found that we were involved in extreme cases of poverty, or sick people that they knew who were not necessarily part of our group but who had a real problem and needed help.

Ian There was one particular family where the church became involved over quite a long period of time.

Nicky There was a woman, recently widowed, who had eleven children, six of whom were not her own. She and her husband had taken on several children from her own sister and brother-in-law who had both died, and then her husband died. So the church paid school fees for the children and we used to provide a food parcel every month. Once the eldest one had finished school we felt it was time to withdraw. But it was for about three years that we helped that particular family.

Ian Were there other specific ways in which you became involved with the community?

Nicky There were deaths. There were situations of extreme poverty where we were asked to help, and we did. We bought coffins and we took the coffin to the home, and then fetched the body from the mortuary with the truck and took it home for burial. It's really just a Christian service, isn't it?

Ian What would you say that you have learnt from your involvement with the St. Raphael's group?

Nicky I've learnt that one mustn't have huge expectations of people. We've given of ourselves and in turn they are willing to give of themselves in the sharing of the Word. But there are also many people who come a few times, thinking that they are going to get something material, and when they find that there isn't a lot of physical anything coming their way, they fall away. We don't know the ripple effects of the teaching that we've given, which they hopefully take home and share with their families. We don't know where that seed blows off to. So we do believe that its worth persevering. We have recently decided that it would be better to go only once a month, and we are encouraging them to meet in their own homes when we don't go, so that the ministry will actually grow. The group has split into three home groups, and we have translated the *Good News Down the Street* course into Zulu for them to study.

Ian You have also helped in getting a feeding scheme established at Dhlokwakhe School, out on the Henley Dam road.

Learning Obedience

Nicky They have a Christian headmistress whom Carol Cassidy and I have known as a good friend for many years. Last year after really bad violence at Taylor's Halt we discovered that there were many children at her school who had been orphaned and were physically in a very bad way. The idea was to start a soup kitchen for these particular children, but the parents were so excited about this when they heard about it that they said, 'Please can all our children have the soup.' So we said, 'Yes, it can be done, but only if you are willing to pay, because those who can afford to pay must pay.' So they have worked out a system, that those who can afford it pay five rand a month per child, and those who can't afford to pay don't, but they have to explain why they can't pay; for example, if they've been unemployed for a long period of time. Each teacher handles her own class of children. So the community themselves are doing everything. They are buying the soup and rice and mealie meal. They burglar-guarded the storeroom windows and the door, and paid for it themselves. They themselves really walked that extra mile, we felt, and were not at all expecting us to hand out everything. They took such a pride in it all. Our church helped them financially for the first six months, but now it is completely in their hands.

I think that a sense of partnership, with us encouraging and enabling something like this, is very important. But I think it is wrong for any school to become too dependent on outside people bringing in things and helping. The people at Dhlokwakhe get the gas cylinders re-filled; they do it themselves. We provided the cylinders and had them filled in the first instance but from there on they have paid each month, and arranged the transport, although we've told them where to go in Pietermaritzburg where they can get it cheaper, because if they get the gas right there where they are, it would cost a lot more. So it's worth taking it into town, and there are plenty of people who've got cars.

Ian But there are some things where our expertise and our contacts can make all the difference.

Nicky Oh definitely. It is a two-way thing. But it is encouraging to see when people really want to take a thing on and run with it on their own.

Ian Is there anything else that has really made an impression on you?

Nicky Well, just that the Lord is gracious to us in this work. There is the amazing way that in spite of my lack of Zulu, because I'm not a great linguist or a good communicator in Zulu, the Lord does use us and deals graciously with us. We can share the Scriptures together because they have a Zulu Bible, and we use an English Bible and it says the same things, so we find that the Lord can speak to us. And so very good relationships are

Learning Obedience

formed. It is a sharing, a relationship of equals. It must be a two-way thing, otherwise it becomes a paternalistic kind of giving, a kind of white guilt which says, 'Oh dear, we've got too much. We'd better give what we can to those who haven't'. It mustn't be like that, because I think that lowers people's self-esteem. So we encourage people to be who they are, and to be thankful for who they are, and to know who they are in Christ. That is really what is important. Unless they know that, they are not going to have self-esteem, no matter how many blankets and shirts and piles of clothes and things we take down and try to give them.

Ian But your involvement with that group is not based on taking down piles of blankets and food. It's based on being part of a Bible study.

Nicky And part of a fellowship. They've taught us a lot too. They've taught us a lot about humility. Although I've been talking about self-esteem, they are incredibly humble when it comes to their relationship with the Lord. They teach us a lot about worship, and praise, and being grateful for what might seem to us to be small things. They are so grateful for things like God's protection in times of trouble. I remember once going to the end of year gathering at the crêche which is just behind the church, and the 'chief mother' who was head of the parents' group was giving thanks for the fact that not one of the children had been injured during that year. Although there had been so much violence around, no children had been hurt. And I thought that was such a wonderful thing to be giving thanks for. It wouldn't occur to us in our church in Hilton at the end of the year to stand up and say, 'Thank you Lord that everyone has been safe this year.' They live so much in a situation of poverty and violence. They learn to be grateful for things that we wouldn't think of. That teaches us a lot. And they sing beautifully, and they praise beautifully, and they are very holy people, some of them, very holy people.

Above all it is the faithfulness of God that comes through. We've seen healings, we've prayed with the people and we've seen God do wonderful things over a long period of time. It's been good. One could so easily become discouraged by thinking that it is such a big thing, and there are such a lot of terrible situations, and so much poverty and damaged relationships but if we are able to do one little bit, it becomes part of something much bigger. I'm sure that in our different little ways, we are all making a difference wherever it is that we go.

… CHAPTER 13

THE IMPORTANCE OF THE LOCAL CHURCH

I often hear people ask, 'Why isn't the church doing this or doing that?' There is always much that the church should be doing, whatever the time and the historical circumstances. But before the church begins to *do* things, it needs to understand what it is called by God to *be*. The church of Jesus Christ receives its calling in and through the cross. The cross reveals the love of God for a suffering and lost world. 'God so loved the world that he gave his only begotten Son ...' (John 3:16) The church is to declare that love, giving and saving, in word and deed.

The primary calling of the church is evangelism. In the great commission which Jesus gave to his disciples in Matthew 28:19 and 20, he said,

'Go therefore and make disciples of all nations, baptizing them in the name of the Father and of the Son and of the Holy Spirit, teaching them to observe all that I have commanded you; and lo, I am with you always, to the close of the age.'

Jesus' primary expectation of his followers was

that they would go and continue the work which he had begun. He taught them to preach the gospel of the kingdom of God, to heal the sick and cast out demons in his name. At the beginning of his own public ministry Jesus came into Galilee, preaching the gospel of God, and saying, 'The time is fulfilled, and the kingdom of God is at hand; repent, and believe in the gospel'. (Mark 1:14-15)

The calling of the church will always be to continue doing the works of Jesus himself. We must do whatever we see Jesus doing. It is important therefore to study the Gospels to see what Jesus himself did, and what he expected his disciples to do, and we must model our own discipleship on this. In John Chapter 14 verse 12 Jesus says, 'Truly, truly, I say to you, he who believes in me will also do the works that I do; and greater works than these will he do, because I go to the Father.'

I was once given some very good advice by a tutor at my theological college. He said that I should not believe anything I was told about the Christian faith unless it could be clearly found to be true in the life and teachings of Jesus himself. This is a principle which is of crucial importance for the whole church, and for every Christian. The church's mission must flow directly from the life and teaching of Jesus Christ. This means also that the cross must be central in the mission of the church, because the cross was central in the life and teaching of Jesus.

The church is often tempted to forsake its primary calling of evangelism. This may happen when life is comfortable and apparently secure, and where the call to forsake the world and follow

The Importance of the Local Church

Jesus is not likely to meet with much response. It may also happen in a situation of crisis and conflict, such as the one in which we find ourselves in South Africa. The danger for the church is that we become so preoccupied with the particular issues and needs of our own society that we fail to remain true to the priorities of Jesus and the gospel.

However, there is another trap into which we Christians have often fallen. The gospel is not only about bringing people to receive forgiveness of sins in Jesus Christ. The gospel is the revelation of God's love for all lost and suffering people. We share in the work of the gospel whenever we serve one another in the love of Jesus. The gospel is both proclamation and loving servanthood and we must not fail to hold these two together. Paul writes in 2 Corinthians 4:5, 'For what we preach is not ourselves, but Jesus Christ as Lord, with ourselves as your servants for Jesus' sake.'

In John chapter 13 we read how on the night that Jesus was betrayed he

> ... rose from supper, laid aside his garments, and girded himself with a towel. Then he poured water into a basin, and began to wash the disciples' feet ... When he had washed their feet, and taken his garments, and resumed his place, he said to them, 'Do you know what I have done to you? ... If I then, your Lord and Teacher, have washed your feet, you also ought to wash one another's feet. For I have given you an example, that you also should do as I have done to you'. (vv. 4, 5, 12, 14, 15)

By learning to become servants for Jesus' sake we learn what it is to truly follow Jesus.

Philippians 2:7 says that Jesus 'emptied himself, taking the form of a servant'. As his disciples we also must be willing to take the form of slaves. In Matthew 20:26-27 Jesus says, 'Whoever would be great among you must be your servant, and whoever would be first among you must be your slave; even as the Son of man came not to be served but to serve, and to give his life as a ransom for many.'

According to Jesus anyone who wants to exercise authority and leadership must be known for their qualities of humility and servanthood.

This has many implications for our understanding of the calling and role of the church. The church's calling is to proclaim the gospel of the kingdom of God, in word and deed, and to be the willing servants of all. The primary concern of the church must always be with people. Jesus focussed on individual people and their particular needs. Mother Teresa of Calcutta has shown us in our own day and age what this means. Her willingness to love the unlovely, the poorest of the poor, the destitute and dying on the streets of Calcutta, has had an extraordinary impact across the world. Malcolm Muggeridge has said of her, 'For me, Mother Teresa of Calcutta embodies Christian love in action. Her face shines with the love of Christ on which her whole life is centred, and her words carry her message to a world which never needed it so much.' Mother Teresa herself said,

'I do not agree with the big way of doing

things. To us what matters is an individual. To get to love the person we must come in close contact with him. I believe in person to person: every person is Christ for me, and since there is only one Jesus, that person is the only one person in the world for me at that moment.'[1]

The church should beware of the 'big way of doing things'. The way of Jesus is person to person. The church is first and foremost a community of people who share the love of Jesus with one another and with those around us. This is why the local church is so important. It is within the local community of believers that person to person caring and serving can take place, day by day, through all the ups and downs of life. The church in South Africa depends for its witness chiefly on thousands of local Christian communities, throughout the country, where although with much weakness and many shortcomings, the commandments of Jesus are being lived out in everyday life. Such communities can have an enormous influence for good by being salt and light in their own local areas. In particular there is a need for Christian communities which will actively seek to break down the effects of apartheid and racial discrimination by their willingness to take costly steps to build relationships with Christians from other race groups and cultures. Some churches may be able to be truly multi-racial, or rather non-racial, by having members drawn from different race groups. Many Anglican churches in the diocese to which I belong are increasingly becoming like this, and throughout the country there is a steady growth in truly non-racial Christian churches and fellowships.

Other churches may find that because of the Group Areas Act it is very difficult for them to lose a specific cultural or racial identity. These churches can work towards building close relationships with churches and Christians in other areas, and towards a real partnership in mission together. This is what our church has committed itself to, in our involvement with Christians in Sweetwaters.

Today much emphasis is being placed on the need to change unjust and oppressive political and economic structures. It is clear to me that the church must be willing to speak out against, and to oppose, unjust systems which exploit and dehumanize people. But the church should be careful to see that such action always flows from, and is rooted in, our person to person ministry. Otherwise the church will find itself pursuing 'the big way of doing things', being involved in the arena of major political and economic power struggles but neglecting that dimension which for Jesus was paramount. To be the servant of all, one must be the servant of particular individuals. It is on the foundation of Christ-like servanthood that we as Christians will be able to speak the mind of Christ to our society. When this is as it should be the church is able to speak with real authority to the modern world. The secular world takes people like Mother Teresa seriously, and listens to what she has to say, because her deeds and her life are the foundation for her words.

The Salvation Army in Britain has similarly won widespread respect, even from those normally

The Importance of the Local Church

hostile to evangelistic Christian groups, because of their work with the poor. The Salvation Army are willing to go anywhere, and especially to areas which other Christian groups find too tough, in order to serve Christ and to preach the gospel.

However, often the media and the wider world do not recognise or even notice the servant ministry of individual Christians and local churches. In the vast majority of cases, in fact, such work and service will remain hidden, unknown and unrecognised. This is where, again, the principle of the cross is at work. Such service is done 'unto Christ', for his sake and for the sake of 'the least of [his] brethren'. (Matt. 25:40) It is done because the love of Christ takes hold of us and leads us to those who are in need. There can be no other truly Christian motive for reaching out in deeds of service and of mercy. Certainly they are not to be done in order to seek popular acclaim or attention.

How then should the local church order its priorities, if it is truly to be controlled and directed by the love of Christ? There are a number of principles which we in our church have found to be important in considering what is involved for the local church to proclaim the gospel in word and deed.

1) The priority of worship and prayer

All action taken in the name of Jesus needs to be rooted in worship and prayer. If this is not happening, then one soon becomes overwhelmed by the needs, the pain and the injustice, and by the many pressures of this kind of life. Effective proclamation of the gospel and true Christ-like servanthood are simply not possible for us unless we have the spiritual resources which Jesus alone can give us. Therefore, we must be spending time with him, in private prayer and corporate worship, on a regular basis.

It is important that members of the church who are engaged in Christian service, particularly in demanding and draining circumstances, should be helped to develop a spirituality which will sustain and direct them in their work. Regular participation in retreats and quiet days is particularly valuable. It is the responsibility of the clergy and church leadership to encourage and help their people to grow in this vital area. Gerard Hughes says, 'Training in prayer should be the main preoccupation and service given by the bishops and clergy to the adult members of the church.'[2]

We see in the life of Jesus an example of the need for the discipline of engagement and disengagement. Jesus often found himself having to teach and to minister to people for long periods of time. He did not make the mistake of being so caught up in meeting human needs that he neglected to take time to maintain his relationship with the Father. He regularly needed to withdraw from the crowds, and even from his own disciples, in order to go to 'a place apart' where he could be alone with the Father. We his disciples today, also need to learn the importance of a balance between our engagement with the needs and problems of our world, and our withdrawal into times of solitude, rest and worship.

2) The centrality of evangelism

I have already said that the primary calling of the church is evangelism. Increasingly it is being recognized that the most effective forms of evangelism are person to person faith sharing and the warmth and outreach of the local church community. Evangelism should be an ongoing part of the life of the local church. There are so many ways in which people can be drawn into the life and witness of the church. Sunday school, youth groups, womens' groups, social events, home groups; all have great potential for welcoming newcomers and enabling them to find a living faith in Christ.

All church groups and organizations need to be encouraged to maintain an openness to newcomers and a desire to draw in those who are outside the life of the church. In particular we have recognized the importance of helping people to be able to share their own faith stories, and to be able 'to account for the hope that is in you.' (1 Peter 3:15) This has been a regular theme in the small group programmes in our church.

In our programme for Sunday morning services we aim to ensure that there are regular occasions when the gospel message is preached, and when people are given the opportunity to make a decision of commitment, or re-commitment, to Christ.

These are occasions of great significance, because of the fruit that is borne in the lives of many people who, through a specific act of response, are enabled to enter into a new and living relationship with the Lord Jesus Christ.

Another effective evangelistic tool which we have used is a course called *Good News Down the Street*, developed by Michael Wooderson.[3] This is a simple course about Jesus Christ, designed for anyone who is interested in deciding for themselves whether the Christian faith is true and relevant to their lives. The idea is that a team of three people, all members of our church, spend about an hour a week with the enquirers, in their own home, for a six-week period. The whole emphasis is on informality, and discussion is allowed to range as widely as the hosts require. This provides a forum in which people can ask questions, air their grievances about the church, clear up misunderstandings, and, hopefully make a decision about Christian faith and discipleship. We have used this course very fruitfully for a number of years in Hilton, and have also translated it into Zulu for use in Sweetwaters.

We must never forget that 'The Son of man came to seek and to save the lost.' (Luke 19:10) This was central to the life and work of Jesus, and it must be central for the church. The lost are those who are separated from Christ, 'having no hope and without God in the world.' (Eph. 2:12) Of course we evangelize not only because people are lost, but because of the huge benefits of knowing Christ personally. Because this is central to the meaning of the gospel, the church must never be content simply to operate programmes of social upliftment. If people are not being drawn to a living faith in Christ through the life and witness of the church, then the church is failing in its mission of obedience to its Lord, Jesus Christ.

3) The call to go to, and be with, those who are in need

Jesus said, 'Go therefore and make disciples of all nations'. (Matt. 28:19) Our physical going is an essential part of what is required for the gospel of Jesus Christ to reach all the nations of the earth. Christians must be willing to go and to be with those who are in need. We have found this to be of particular importance in Sweetwaters. Material gifts alone are not enough to bring the love of Christ to people who are suffering. It is usually better for someone to go empty handed and give an hour or more of their time, than to simply send a gift of food or money. A gift alone does not create a relationship. If a relationship is established first, then both sides are able to give to one another. One-sided giving does not bring about healing and reconciliation where there is distrust, fear, anger and guilt. In many cases one-sided giving can in fact increase the anger and the hurt. The response of black people to gifts, given by well-meaning white Christians far away, may well be one of accepting the gift but being embittered towards the giver, because no attempt has been made to understand or deal with the causes of the people's poverty and suffering. We trample on people's dignity if we treat them as objects for our charity, and if we do this it is likely that they will show anger and bitterness towards us, instead of the gratitude that we might expect.

So often we have seen that the first thing that we need to do for people in Sweetwaters is not to bring gifts or to organize a project for them. It is simply to go and to be with them, to get to know them, to understand their concerns and needs, and to allow them also to get to know us and to share their lives with us. Then there is a giving and receiving, the love of Christ begins to be shared, and true reconciliation can take place. Reconciliation is costly, and it cannot be bought. True reconciliation happens when two people find that the love of Christ binds them together, and this is something that often is clearly miraculous and supernatural. God is able to break down the barriers between people from vastly different social backgrounds and circumstances, when they meet together and open themselves to one another through a common commitment to Jesus Christ. This has been our experience, over and over again.

4) A balance between spiritual ministry and practical care

I have in previous chapters described how our work in Sweetwaters has combined both spiritual ministry and practical care. There are serious problems with a style of evangelism which seeks to bring people to 'a decision for Christ', but which does not seriously address their physical needs.

The Importance of the Local Church

This is particularly true when those people are living in appalling poverty. Such attempts at evangelism have clearly not come to grips with the demands of the love of Christ in such circumstances. The Epistle of James says,

> What does it profit, my brethren, if a man says he has faith but has not works? Can his faith save him? If a brother or sister is ill-clad and in lack of daily food, and one of you says to them, 'Go in peace, be warmed and filled,' without giving them the things needed for the body, what does it profit? (James 2:14–16)

It is also not sufficient to provide material relief for people's needs – food, blankets, clothing, and so on – and not to do any more than this. The spiritual dimension of the relationship between the 'haves' and the 'have-nots' of this world is fraught with risk. This is partly because of the guilt and fear, which often motivate those who are materially well-off, and the possibility of bitterness and anger amongst the 'have-nots'. It is also difficult for the materially rich to recognize that they are often the ones who are spiritually poor, and who have much to learn from the weak and helpless of this world.

Nonetheless, it is vital that Christians take the risk of actively sharing their faith and thereby bringing whatever encouragement and help they can. It is faith that produces hope, which in turn brings joy and the strength to persevere. In Christ we have a true faith and a sure hope, which is able to transform every human circumstance and need.

5) The need for community

The New Testament does not know of a type of Christian life which is lived in isolation from other Christians. To be a Christian is to be a member of the community of God's people in Jesus Christ. The local church is the local community of Christian people; it is a group of people who live out their faith together in one specific setting or place.

Every member of the local church has their own gifts and ministries, and all of these together make up the whole life of the church. Some are evangelists, some teachers, some prophets, some have pastoral gifts, some are administrators. In our church we have found that some are able to preach and teach the faith, while others look after orphans and widows; one person is responsible for the maintenance of the Sweetwaters truck, while another runs a weekly prayer meeting. Some members of the church are called to the Sweetwaters work, but others are involved elsewhere, in visiting the local prison, in hospitals and schools and so on.

In this way the local church is able to be a living Christian community. There is day by day support and care for one another within the church and, at the same time, a daily reaching out into the world. Where individual Christians are cut off from the local church and are trying to live out a Christian calling in isolation from the church, they soon find themselves in need of the wide measure of support which the church can offer. They also can easily lose the balance that comes from regular fellowship with other Christians who have different gifts and emphases. I doubt whether there is any substitute for the support and care of a strong and lively local church in the life of any Christian who is seeking to actively live out their faith in the modern world.

6) The church is called to be an agent of reconciliation

In the deep divisions of South African society the church has a unique role as a bridge-builder and reconciler. Bishop Michael Nuttall, the Anglican Bishop of Natal, has said that,

'... the church should not be attached to any partisan point of view or political stance, but should seek to be a prophetic voice in society, and attempt to effect a bridge-building and reconciling role where there has been unnecessary and tragic conflict and violence'.[4]

This is the situation in which the church finds itself in South Africa at present. In Sweetwaters the church has been literally in the middle ground as fighting and killing goes on all around. One Sunday, Bishop Ken Hallowes was taking a service of Holy Communion in the Anglican church of St. Gabriel's, Nxamalala, in Sweetwaters. The church is in the middle of a valley, and while Bishop Ken and a small group of worshippers were praying, a battle broke out in the valley around them. They could hear the sound of the fighting, with one group on one side of the valley and the other group on the other side. The church was literally in the middle, weak and physically unable to stop the conflict, but able to be there as a sign of the presence of Christ; and able to pray, in the midst of the war.

Often the church will find that it is able to bring opposing sides together to listen to one another and hopefully to find common ground and to resolve problems, hurts and misunderstandings. Mbulelo Hina, an evangelist with the African Enterprise team in Pietermaritzburg says,

> The role of Christians is to bridge the gulf between people. They do that by exposing them to one another. If there is tension between figureheads, for example, the Christian would move into that gap, start the dialogue, clarify matters and focus on things they have in common. The major role of the Christian would be to act as conciliator.[5]

7) The local church should acknowledge the role of prophetic ministry

St. Paul speaks often in the New Testament about the role of prophets in the church. The church has never found prophetic ministry easy to handle. Nonetheless prophets have a most important role to play in the church. Paul esteemed the ministry of prophets very highly. In 1 Corinthians 12 verse 28 he writes, 'And God has appointed in the church first apostles, second prophets, third teachers, then workers of miracles, then healers, helpers, administrators . . .'

The role of the prophet is to call the church to obedience to God. This may involve bringing words of encouragement and proclamation, and also words of challenge and even of rebuke. Because God's ways are not our ways, and his thoughts are not our thoughts, the prophet will often find himself in a lonely and unpopular place as he seeks to be obedient in challenging the church to hear what God is saying to them. The prophet is likely to strike at all the complacency, idleness and indifference within the church, and to call the people of God to purify their lives, to repent of their sins and to bear fruits that befit repentance, as John the Baptist did in Luke Chapter 3. John the Baptist is a clear example of the Biblical model of a prophet.

We should not be surprised if we find prophets appearing in the church today. But what do we do with them, when they do appear in our midst? In the local church, the work of the prophet is to call the people to be faithful and obedient to God, in specific and sometimes very personal ways. For obvious reasons many local churches do not give much attention to the ministry of prophets. However we have found this ministry to be very important in bringing about a willingness to hear the Lord's call, and to obey, often in costly and demanding ways. Prophets can be recognized not just by their words, but primarily by their life, which should be distinctively Christ-like and holy. The words of a prophet must be carefully weighed by other members of the church (see 1 Cor. 14:29), and especially by the elders or those in leadership.

Not all prophetic ministry will necessarily be of value, and sometimes the prophet may himself, or herself, need to be rebuked or corrected. But the dangers and problems that can arise from this ministry should not cause us to deny it altogether. Prophets need the local church, for support, encouragement and discernment. The local church needs prophets, to keep it awake to the voice of the Spirit of God, and faithful in being doers, and not just hearers of God's word.

8) The local church should stand for justice and truth

I have written about this already in Chapter 10 of this book. The leadership of the local church have a particular responsibility to see that the church does not avoid being involved in issues which affect both the local area and the wider society, and which require a response in the light of biblical standards and principles. There is always a temptation for the church to want to avoid its prophetic role in society, and to seek instead a more comfortable role of conformity with the *status quo*. This is not the way that Jesus chose in his own society, and it is not what he expects of his disciples today. He expects his disciples to be the light that confronts the darkness, the salt that gives a distinct taste to the meat, and which preserves it and stops it from going rotten. There is thus also a need for the congregation to be regularly made aware of the implications of the gospel for their society. The challenge for the church is to develop a Christian mind and Christian values,

The Importance of the Local Church 171

and to act upon these, in obedience to God rather than in the fear of man.

9) In the local church people are renewed in faith and hope

South Africa has, over the past few years, often been a deeply depressing place to be. The bad news has gone on and on, and at times, outside of the church, there has been very little good news at all. In a normal society one can live with a measure of bad news, because there are many positive aspects to life, many pleasures and rewarding activities, through which one is refreshed and renewed to face the challenges of life. In South Africa the sense of grief and pain and frustration has often been overwhelming. In these circumstances the church must become a place where people can find healing, cleansing and strength to face the challenges of the coming week.

The only way in which the church can be such a place is through a determination to fix our eyes on God, and to worship him as the sovereign Lord of all creation. In the Psalms there is a strong emphasis on praise and worship and on the need to turn to God in times of need.

> God is our refuge and strength,
>   a very present help in trouble.
> Therefore we will not fear though the earth
>   should change,
>   though the mountains shake in the heart
>   of the sea.
>
> (Psalm 46:1–2)

The Psalms constantly remind us of the character of God; his greatness and power, his steadfast love and faithfulness to those who trust in him. We have tried to model our worship on the attitudes which we find in the Psalms, and have found this to be most relevant in our South African situation. The Book of Psalms is the prayer and worship book of the Bible, and it provides the basis for the worship of God's people in every age and circumstance, particularly in times of trouble and distress. From the Psalms we learn to begin our worship with praise and thanksgiving. We often encourage people to thank God openly in the services for all his gifts to us. This provides a positive focus at the beginning of our worship. We then allow time for reflection and confession, so that all may be assured of God's forgiveness in Christ.

We have learned to spend time in silence before God, allowing him time to bring his peace, quietness and rest to the hearts of the people. We also encourage people to listen to the Holy Spirit, and to bring words from the Lord to the congregation, through which we may sense that God is speaking to us either corporately or to particular individuals in the church. All this is built into the framework of the Anglican liturgical tradition, with its emphasis on the Holy Communion as the sacrament which binds the church together in unity and through which we are renewed week by week for Christian service and witness.

In these and many other ways the worship of the local church becomes a place where people are renewed in faith and prayer, and are enabled by the Lord to go out in his name and to continue to serve him, often in difficult circumstances. God

The Importance of the Local Church

pours out his Holy Spirit upon his people when they are gathered together with a sincere desire to glorify his name and seek his holy presence. When Jesus Christ is exalted as Lord of Lords, and King of Kings, then faith is built up, hope is renewed and the vision of the kingdom of God is re-kindled among the people of God.

> Then the seventh angel blew his trumpet, and there were loud voices in heaven, saying, 'The kingdom of the world has become the kingdom of our Lord and of his Christ, and he shall reign for ever and ever.' And the twenty-four elders who sit on their thrones before God fell on their faces and worshipped God, saying, 'We give thanks to thee, Lord God Almighty, who art and wast, that thou hast taken thy great power and begun to reign. The nations raged, but thy wrath came, and the time for the dead to be judged, for rewarding thy servants, the prophets and saints, and those who fear thy name, both small and great, and for destroying the destroyers of the earth.' (Rev. 11:15–18)

In the worship of the local church these words become charged with truth and reality, and God is able to inspire his people to go out and to proclaim the gospel of Jesus Christ in word and deed, and to face both the cost and the opposition. Discouragement and depression flee away, and faith, hope and courage are renewed, again and again. Together we declare our faith, we sing, and we know that it is true that, no matter what the circumstances around us, 'our God reigns'.

CHAPTER 14
THE CHALLENGE OF THE POOR

In the wintertime, on the road that runs between Hilton and Sweetwaters, you may often see a line of women walking, carrying on their heads large bundles of firewood. Firewood is very hard to find in Sweetwaters, while it is abundant in Hilton. So groups of women come to Hilton to gather whatever wood they can find, and then set off, walking five or ten miles, each with a bundle of wood on their head. White people drive past in their cars, see the women walking, and know why they are doing this, but how many ever think further about what is involved in this for these women? The long walk, the heavy burden, the many hours, all for a bit of firewood to cook some food and to warm the family on a bitter winter's night.

Gilbert Lukau is the catechist at St. Michael's Church, on the boundary between Sweetwaters and the white suburb of Winterskloof. He is an old man who has faithfully served and pastored the people of his parish for many many years. He does not have a car or a telephone, and he generally walks wherever he has to go. He often comes to see me at our church in Hilton if there

The Challenge of the Poor

is a problem or something with which I might be able to help him. One morning he came in to see me. He had a number of problems, so we talked for a while, and then I asked him where he was going next. He told me that a regional Mothers' Union gathering had been postponed and he was on his way to Cedara to tell his congregation there. Cedara is about five miles from Hilton. Gilbert was planning to walk over ten miles simply to tell a small group of people that a meeting had been postponed. I said to him, 'Come on, I'll take you in the car.' We drove round to Cedara, Gilbert found the person to whom he needed to pass on his message, and we were back in Hilton in less than half an hour. Such is the difference between the way of life of a white resident of Hilton and a black resident of Sweetwaters. Telephones, motor cars, stoves, fridges, electricity, piped water and sewage disposal, all make an enormous difference to our lives. We in Hilton take these things for granted. What idea do we have of what life must be like for those who do not have such things? Do we even care?

If you go to a crêche in Sweetwaters you will see many children dressed in what can only be described as rags. Very few will have shoes upon their feet. My wife and I have been concerned that we buy good shoes for our own two young children, so that their feet will grow properly. Good children's shoes are expensive, but for us this is an expense which we regard as necessary and important. It is hard for us to imagine ourselves in the position where to have any shoes at all would be a luxury. Many black people are more than happy to wear a pair of shoes that a white person has thrown away because they are worn out.

I have been into homes – mud huts – in Sweetwaters where the only furniture has been wooden boxes and planks, plus an old cupboard or two that would long since have been thrown out by any white family. On the floor there is only newspaper – there are no carpets or flooring tiles. The roof is made up of old rusty corrugated iron tied down with wire. Yet the people who live here are not ashamed of their poverty. They have a simple dignity, and they welcome a visitor with all the graciousness and warmth of any wealthy white family. In fact often in visiting white homes I have been confronted with large security gates and vicious dogs, especially if I should decide to just 'drop in', and not to phone first in order to warn people that I am planning to visit.

Those who are poor, crippled and forgotten are often simply not able, on their own, to deal with the problems of life in the way in which white people of education and means simply take for granted. An example of this is the story of Richard Nkomo, which was reported in *The Natal Witness* on 24th July, 1989. The story read:

MAN FINALLY GETS HIS I.D. AFTER 3-YEAR WAIT

Tears of joy welled in the eyes of a Sweetwaters man when he received his ID book after an almost three-year wait. All Mr Richard Madondo Nkomo could say was 'ngiyabonga' when women from the Church of the Ascension in Hilton handed over his document. 'When I got my book, I thought I was dreaming,' he said.

Mr Nkomo, who is paralysed in the left arm and leg, first applied for his ID in November, 1986, with the hope that he could then apply for a disability pension. Nothing happened. After an 18 month wait he went again to Vulindlela and filled out a new form. He was told that the ID number he had furnished was the cause of the delay and that it seemed to be someone else's number. In March he applied again.

Mr Nkomo had been told that further problems had arisen because he could not remember his date of birth and he was not on the population register. Mr Nkomo thought he was about 60, but was not sure and there was no member of the family to verify this.

Mr Nkomo has been able to survive without an income only through the help of a neighbour who has fed, clothed and cared for him since he has been in the area.

'I am going to apply for a disability pension and I hope I don't have to wait as long,' he said. Asked what he would do once he received his pension money he said: 'I am going to put the money in the bank. But first I want to buy a bed, some blankets and some food.'

Some years ago I went with Graham Beggs to visit an old couple who lived in a simple home high up in one of the valleys that spread out from the main road through Sweetwaters. The man was a retired teacher. He showed us with great pride some old photographs of himself and his colleagues at the school near Pietermaritzburg where he had taught for many years. Now he and his wife were living, on a tiny pension, in a small mud house far away from the bustle of the city. Yet crime and social disturbance had reached even this forgotten corner; this lonely, helpless, dignified couple. Youths had come and broken into their house. They had smashed the windows and stolen what little they could find. But the worst blow, as the old man said to us, was that 'they took my radio'. 'They have stolen my radio,' he said over and over again. His one link with the outside world was gone, and he could never replace it.

It is necessary to enter the world of those who live in poverty in order to begin to understand the nature of the world that has come to be, the world that we are living in. It is a world which asks very serious questions of anyone who claims to be a disciple of Jesus Christ. Mostly, I suspect, Christians who are born and grow up in a rich western environment find it extremely difficult to think seriously about these issues. They are complex, and there is no easy solution. But they also demand a response from every single Christian, if the Christian message is to have any real meaning and credibility in the modern world.

Further, it has become clear to me that the problem is getting worse, not better. The gap between the rich and the poor is increasing not diminishing. The rich *are* getting richer and the poor *are* getting poorer. Increasingly, western lifestyles are accepting advanced technology as part of what is necessary for daily living even though this technology is enormously costly. Video recorders, fax machines, microwave ovens and so on

The Challenge of the Poor

are thus not regarded as luxuries. Yet when compared to the needs of most families in Africa these are outrageously expensive items. To find people spending huge sums of money on BMWs, Porsches and Ferraris, when one knows first hand of the suffering of those who live out their daily lives in the most dreadful poverty, cannot but raise all kinds of questions and challenges.

Medical technology is but one area where this increasing gap of expectations and material resources is evident. The cost of drugs, scans, and high-tech diagnostic and surgical equipment has increased dramatically in the last ten years. The benefits of such technology and medication are not to be underestimated, for they have brought help and healing to many, many people. Yet even here questions need to be asked. What about the thousands upon thousands of people who lack even the most basic medical care and facilities? Although there are doctors available to black people, as well as a large hospital in Edendale, many medical problems amongst the poor in our area are simply never treated. For many it is only when a condition becomes serious that treatment will be sought, and often by then it is too late. Also even then, getting many miles to hospital or to the doctor presents a major problem, long queues are the order of the day, and specialist care is unlikely to be available.

A short report in *The Natal Witness* of 24th October, 1990 was headed, 'Economic gap is intolerable'. The report read as follows:

> The gap between rich and poor in South Africa has become intolerable, says Old Mutual chief operations officer Gerhard van

Niekerk. Addressing the national congress of the Afrikaanse Handelsinstituut in Durban, Van Niekerk said the unrealistic economic expectations of the general population would have to be scaled down. 'Re-distribution of wealth within the context of a growing economy is essential. The discrepancies in South Africa's patterns of income distribution are among the world's worst,' he said.

This short report points to one of the most serious issues in South Africa today. It is an issue which many of the 'rich' try to avoid having to face. But it simply must be faced because, as Gerhard van Niekerk says, there can be no escaping the need for redistribution of wealth within such a situation. We need to face, also, the fact that the South African economic gap is only a small scale reflection of the global gap between the rich 'first world' and the poor 'third world'. These are not merely South African issues; they are global issues.

The Anglican Diocese of Natal owns two farms. One called Springvale is in the Ixopo area. The other, Modderspruit, is near Ladysmith in Northern Natal. At the Diocesan Synod in 1988 the following figures were given to the Synod in a Diocesan report on these two properties:

	Springvale Rural	**Modderspruit** Essentially urban
De facto resident population	656	2,930
Mean monthly cash income of sample households	R215	R662

The Challenge of the Poor

| Local employment opportunities | 80% of all earned income of households is in the form of wage remittances from migrant workers | Much higher proportion of total income derived from permanently resident workers. |

The striking contrast between a rural and an essentially urban black area can be seen here. The monthly income of a household in Modderspruit of R662 per month was not a lot of money, even in 1988. But the R215 per month for a household in Springvale is simply appalling. R215 is far less than the average white household would have spent per month on food alone in 1988. I estimate that in 1988 my own family of two adults and two children was spending between R400 and R500 per month on food.

These vast differences in incomes and living standards between rich and poor are a recipe for conflict and social upheaval. Poverty leads to crime and numerous other social problems. The Christian cannot be indifferent to poverty, especially when it is on his or her own doorstep. Christians must heed the voice of the poor. They must be willing to act in compassion and in the knowledge that God's will for our world is that there should be a just sharing of its resources. We know that it is the will of God that no-one should have to live in such poverty that they lack even adequate food, water and clothing, and a roof over their heads. What should our response be to the challenge of the poor? This is not an easy question to answer. The response of each individual will depend upon their own abilities and circumstances. But of one thing I am certain; that in every Christian there must be a response.

Gustavo Gutierrez says, 'If today we are not somehow committed to the poor we are in danger of living far from God.'[1]

Gutierrez is a pastor-theologian at the Catholic University of Lima in Peru. In an address at the Lambeth Conference in England in 1988, Gutierrez spoke from his own experience as a member of a poor family and a pastor of a community of the poor. He said:

> To be poor is a way to know, a way to make friends, to love, to speak. The poor are rich as persons, but their situation is poverty and death. To be a Christian is to enter into the world of the poor. We are committed to the poor if we have friends among the poor. Because to have friends among the poor is to share our life with them.[2]

Our response should be therefore to seek, in whatever way we can, to enter into personal contact and relationships with those who are poor. We can do this whether we live in Africa or South America, or in Europe or North America. It is important to broaden our awareness of the conditions and the facts concerning poverty in our world. It is even more important to see these conditions for ourselves. We are then able to help, to give and to serve, in ways which will be appropriate for those in need, and practically feasible for us.

A second aspect to our Christian response should be a firm commitment to live simply and to give

The Challenge of the Poor

generously. Some years ago when we were living in Sheffield in England, my wife and I were challenged one Christmas to sign a pledge on a small poster produced by Christian Aid, and to put it up in a place in our home where we could see it in the year that lay ahead. It read, 'Remembering that many in our human family live in overwhelming poverty, I pledge myself to live and give in ways that will help them.'

Christian Aid made some suggestions on this poster. They asked that, on Christmas Eve or on another day in the week before Christmas, Will you:

1. Do without a meal or meals, or eat very simply.
2. Think of those to whom that experience is a daily one.
3. Give what you save to Christian Aid, direct or through your local church so that projects to help the oppressed and hungry can be carried out.
4. Find out about the changes needed to create a world that is more fair and just.
5. Resolve to think about a fitting 'life-style' for Christians in today's world, and try to work it out in the New Year.

I think that these are appropriate and helpful suggestions. It has been said that we should 'live simply, that others may simply live'. This means asking ourselves before we buy something, 'Do I really need this?' The western world is gripped by materialism and greed. We can provide an example of a different way of living by not buying some of the things which we might like to have, but which we can do without.

My wife and I have wrestled a great deal with this issue of seeking a simple lifestyle. We are committed to trying to live out a fitting lifestyle for Christians in today's world. We are very conscious of the fact that, although we do not consider ourselves to be rich, we nonetheless live extremely well in comparison with the vast majority of people in Sweetwaters. It is therefore necessary for us to think very carefully about the way we spend our money. We have found that in general it is better to buy quality products, things that will last, rather than cheaper products. As a friend once said to us, 'I simply can't afford to buy things that are cheap.' We also feel that, in order to live lives of service to others, we need to look after ourselves. We need to eat good and healthy food, but through discipline to avoid the over-eating which is so common in western society.

For us, going to the occasional symphony concert or movie is something which is important for our own health and well-being. These things may be luxuries, but they are nonetheless important for us if we are to survive in this work. We need to be 'normal' and yet different, those who are able to enjoy life, to go out for a meal occasionally, to listen to music and watch sporting events, but not those who are totally caught up in these things without being mindful of the needs and suffering of others. This is not an easy balance to find. For us the community of the local church is a great help to us in working towards this balance. Some in the church are intensely concerned with the poor and the demands of the gospel. They need to be helped

The Challenge of the Poor

not to take themselves too seriously, to relax and to yield their concerns to God. Others are easily caught up in the concerns and pleasures of the world, and they need the prophetic challenge of others to help them to be faithful disciples of the Lord Jesus.

To sum up, here are a few principles which we have found helpful.

1. Enter into personal contact and relationship with the poor.
2. Prayerfully consider the teaching of Scripture about money and Christian giving.
3. Give generously. In our parish we teach the biblical standard of tithing. However, God may often lead us to give more than a tithe (one tenth of our income). It is a good principle of faith to give more than we can humanly afford, because this leads us to a greater dependence upon God for the provision of our needs.
4. Live simply. Resist extravagance. Give away the things that you have but do not need. Ask before you buy something, 'Do I really need this? What is God saying to me about this?'
5. Sometimes it is valuable for us to observe times of fasting or abstinence. Apart from the spiritual value of this, it also enables us to understand more fully what it is like to go without some of the things which we so easily take for granted.
6. In our spending we should always be mindful of the need to care for the world which God has made. Both rich and poor

suffer because of pollution and the destruction of the environment. But it is generally the poor who suffer more than the rich.

Jesus said, 'You always have the poor with you.' (Matt. 26:11) This can never be an excuse for us to be indifferent to the poor. Let us be reminded that Jesus also said in Matthew 25:35–40,

'I was hungry and you gave me food, I was thirsty and you gave me drink, I was a stranger and you welcomed me, I was naked and you clothed me, I was sick and you visited me, I was in prison and you came to me . . . Truly I say to you, as you did it to one of the least of these my brethren, you did it to me.'

Mother Teresa has said:

We all long for heaven where God is, but we have it in our power to be in heaven with him right now – to be happy with him at this very moment. But being happy with him now means:

loving as he loves
helping as he helps
giving as he gives
serving as he serves
rescuing as he rescues
being with him twenty-four hours
touching him in his distressing disguise.[3]

CHAPTER 15
THE INWARD JOURNEY

It was a Saturday afternoon in September, 1988. The last few months had been exhausting for me personally. The situation in Sweetwaters was bad, with ongoing violence and killings. We had recently had a burglary at our church in Hilton, in which considerable damage was done to the church offices – curtains ripped down, doors and windows and cupboards smashed, the church's crockery and cutlery stolen, and so on. As well as this I had been involved in a number of missions in other churches in Natal and I was increasingly aware that I had taken on too much. I was feeling the strain.

The phone rang. It was the military chaplain from Durban. A young national serviceman had been killed on the border. His parents were staying with friends in a farming area about half an hour's drive from Hilton. Would I be prepared to go and tell them what had happened? Otherwise the chaplain would have to drive up from Durban himself. Naturally I said that I would go.

It was a sunny spring afternoon, and the Natal countryside was looking as restful and as beautiful as ever. I did not feel restful however. I felt a tense apprehension of the task that lay ahead of me. An only son, an only child, nearly twenty-one years of age, tragically killed just before his national service was due to be completed. And I had to break the news to his parents. When they saw me walking down the path to the house in my clerical collar they immediately knew that something was wrong. I spent nearly two hours with them that afternoon, trying to comfort two distraught parents who just could not come to terms with this awful thing that had happened to them. Eventually I felt able to leave them with their friends, and to get back in the car and drive home. As I drove I reflected bitterly: this was the reality of life in South Africa.

The next afternoon something strange happened to me. I was taking a Zulu Eucharist in the church in Hilton. I became aware of a feeling that I was losing control, in a way that I had never felt before. I felt dizzy and weak; my mind seemed to be spinning, and I could not get a grip on things. I went home to bed, and got up an hour or so later feeling a little better.

The week that followed was the annual Diocesan clergy retreat. On the first afternoon of the retreat I was able to share my experience with a fellow priest who also happened to be a psychologist. He said he thought that I was experiencing the symptoms of post-traumatic shock, and he suggested some tranquillizers to help me through this. I knew something was wrong with me; I had never needed to take tranquillizers before.

Gradually I came to realize what had happened – I had simply pushed myself too far, and the events of Saturday afternoon had been the straw that broke the camel's back. Fortunately I was

The Inward Journey

due shortly to take two and a half months leave, from mid-October to the end of December. Much of this time was spent in England, and this was a time for me to begin to reverse the process of exhaustion and to embark upon a journey of inner healing which has changed many of my ideas about the church and my own calling as an ordained minister.

One Sunday while I was in England I attended an evening service at St. Andrew's, Chorleywood, where Bishop David Pytches is the Rector, and where there is a well-known ministry of healing, particularly inner healing. Towards the end of this service Bishop David asked those who would like to receive prayer and ministry to move to the front of the church. I knew that I needed prayer and I must have been among the first to go forward. A couple from the church prayed with me, very sensitively and gently. They asked me what I wanted prayer for. I described my exhaustion, and my need for God to heal me of much hurt and pain relating to the situation in South Africa. I knelt down and they began to pray for me. As they prayed I began to sob, something which is very unusual for me. I cried and cried, until I felt that I did not need to cry any more. All this took place quietly in a corner of the church; I doubt whether any one else knew what was happening. Later I realized that what I had been expressing was grief, a deep and prolonged grief over what was happening to my country. With this grief there was also an anger. I was profoundly angry that so much evil had been allowed to flourish and to destroy many, many lives. I needed to acknowledge and to deal with this grief and this anger in order to be healed, and through the ministry of the Holy Spirit at St. Andrew's, Chorleywood that process of healing took a major step forward.

When we immerse ourselves in situations of great human need and suffering, we will be changed by what we experience. These things affect us deeply, and by the Spirit of God they can be used to make us more Christ-like, more fully human. But for this to happen, there often needs to be a breaking, a shattering of the whole self, the old hard shell, so that a new soft heart may be born in us. This is a painful process. It is a dying and a being reborn. It is the way of the cross, which alone leads to the resurrection and to life. Jesus said,

> 'Truly, truly, I say to you, unless a grain of wheat falls into the earth and dies, it remains alone; but if it dies, it bears much fruit. He who loves his life loses it, and he who hates his life in this world will keep it for eternal life.' (John 12:24–25)

To be broken is often the first step towards being healed, and towards finding one's true self. Yet brokenness and weakness is something that we fear and resist. I had always needed and worked hard to be strong and in control. Now I had to discover in a new way what it was to be weak, and to know my need of God. In this weakness God was very near to me. I knew that without him I would be totally lost. I simply had to abide daily in him. Jesus said, 'I am the vine, you are the branches. He who abides in me, and I in him,

The Inward Journey

he it is that bears much fruit, for apart from me you can do nothing.' (John 15:5)

When we are brought to the end of ourselves, we find that it is true that apart from Jesus we can do nothing. It is in our weakness that his strength is made perfect. Paul wrote in 2 Corinthians 12:9–10:

> He said to me, 'My grace is sufficient for you, for my power is made perfect in weakness.' ... For the sake of Christ, then, I am content with weaknesses, insults, hardships, persecutions, and calamities; for when I am weak, then I am strong.

This has been a hard lesson to learn, and I do not say that I have fully learnt it yet. But I have learnt a great deal about myself, and indeed also about God. I have learnt about the faithfulness of God, no matter what life may bring. I have also learnt that God is always at work in us to make us more and more Christ-like. This involves dying to all those old habits which are based on self – self-reliance, self-pity, self-seeking, self-aggrandisement. This also involves discovering the truth about ourselves. When Jesus was led by the Holy Spirit into the wilderness after his baptism in the Jordan, it was so that in that place he would face up to the deceptions and wrong motives with which Satan sought to entrap him. The work of the Holy Spirit is to lead us into all truth, to purify our inner drives and motivations, and so to make us more wholly yielded to God and to his will.

Thus I have had to learn much about myself.

The need in me to be successful and to be recognized and approved by others has been deeply challenged. I have discovered that I do not have to prove myself. God has graciously accepted me, unconditionally, as I am, and he is working out his good purpose for me, in me and through me. I can be completely satisfied in this. I can also be gentle with myself, because God does not expect me to be responsible for more than I am able to cope with. So often I had felt weighed down by the burden of what I saw as my responsibilities. I tended to push myself, and to push other people in the church, in order to fulfil certain expectations. I wanted the church to grow, to be involved in mission, in evangelism, in serving the poor, in effective pastoral care, in every-member ministry, in prayer, in vibrant weekly worship, and so on. But where were all of these expectations coming from? I began to realize that God did not expect me to be the perfect pastor, and to do all these things which I had read about in countless books on church growth, power evangelism and other such topics! God wanted me simply to be *myself*, Ian Cowley, with all my weaknesses as well as my strengths. I needed to focus, not on the burden of unending responsibilities and goals, but on the daily pleasure and satisfaction of doing those things which God gives me to do, in the strength and grace which he provides.

I also had to realize that the Church of the Ascension was not *my* church. The church belongs to the Lord Jesus Christ. He is the head of the church, and he is able to sustain it, direct it and enable it to fulfil his will and purpose. All that God requires of me is a daily listening to him and daily obedience

The Inward Journey

to his will for me. There was a great release for me in grasping these truths, which I had known intellectually for a long time, but only now were they truly transforming my inner motivations and attitudes. In my sense of weakness I had no option but to hand over the church to Jesus.

I was not the only one who found these times very testing indeed. Bishop Michael Nuttall in his charge to the Synod of the Diocese of Natal in August, 1990 had this to say:

> As I look back over the two years that have elapsed since our last session of Synod, I freely confess that I have found them an incredibly stretching and even stressful time. My sense is that church leaders, both ordained and lay, are stretched to the limit by the pressures, both outward and inward, which come upon us. It is not surprising that some come unstuck in emotional or marital breakdown. We have to come back to basics, and one of these is the need for a balanced spirituality with an authentic combination of prayer and action, of retreat and engagement, and above all of waiting for the Lord to renew our strength. We have to live with Elijah's paradox: if you would show yourself, hide yourself.
>
> Let me illustrate what I mean by my reference to the stretching and the stress. The worsening violence in Natal has been an ever-present reality. Some people will find it hard to believe that we live in one of the most violent societies in the world. Where else, other than places like the Lebanon and

Sri Lanka, have there been as many as 3,000 deaths in civil conflict in the space of three and a half years? I have feared deeply for our clergy ministering directly in this conflict situation, and I have immense admiration for their tenacity and devotion, and for their corporate decision not to be members of any of the political organisations involved.

Bishop Michael then spoke of the murder of Victor Afrikander, and some of the other painful and stressful events of the past two years and he went on to say:

Who is sufficient for all these things, and for more besides which could also have been mentioned? None of us is. It is better to be open about our weakness and vulnerability as we face the many demands and pressures in our needy world, and even in the life of the church. We were never promised an easy road. What we were, and are, promised is strength for the journey. This is the clear teaching of St. Paul. 'The Spirit helps us,' he says, 'in our weakness.' (Rom. 8:26) 'We have this treasure in earthen vessels, to show that the transcendent power belongs to God and not to us.' (2 Cor. 4:7) When contemplating his own vulnerability and his utter dependence, because of it, upon the grace of God, he said tersely: 'When I am weak, then I am strong.' (2 Cor. 12:10)

Through this time I learned much about my own

weakness and dependence. Yet, looking back I can say that this was a time of healing, of strengthening, and of growth. I can thank God for this time, because of what he did in me through it. Finding our strength in God and discovering our true dependence on him is not easy for us. Yet it is essential to spiritual growth. Gerard Hughes says that 'our lives must be . . . a constant struggle to change the direction of our lives from preoccupation with our own security to letting God be our only security'.[1]

My understanding of what the ordained ministry means for me has also undergone a significant change. I found that I had been set free to a considerable degree from the need to prove myself and to be successful. I could trust God for the life and ministry of the church. I was, and I am still, learning to be content with weakness, because in my weakness God's strength is able to be at work. So what now seemed to matter most to me was to deepen my knowledge of God. My goals in life were now to learn to live at peace with God, to look after myself, and to love and serve others, especially my own family, to the best that I am able. Spirituality and reflection now seemed to be more important for me as an ordained priest than success and growth in the church. Instead of seeking the responsibilities of leadership, I wanted instead simply to be faithful in prayer, in teaching and preaching the Word of God and in pastoring God's people. There would be less activity and busyness, more quietness, reading and praying. Instead of producing results, I now wanted above all to live by prayer, and thus by the strength and grace of God. During this time I was often reminded of the words of Isaiah 40:28–31. These words have come true in my own life.

> Have you not known? Have you not heard?
> The Lord is the everlasting God,
>   the Creator of the ends of the earth.
> He does not faint or grow weary,
>   his understanding is unsearchable.
> He gives power to the faint,
>   and to him who has no might he increases strength.
> Even youths shall faint and be weary,
>   and young men shall fall exhausted;
> but they who wait for the LORD shall renew their strength,
>   they shall mount up with wings like eagles,
> they shall run and not be weary,
>   they shall walk and not faint.

CHAPTER 16
THE WAY FORWARD – OUR GOD REIGNS

Our God reigns. Jesus Christ died on the cross, although he was innocent of any crime, and on the third day he rose again. Without the cross, there would have been no resurrection. As Christians we believe that through his death and resurrection Jesus has conquered sin and death and all that is evil, and through faith we share in that victory. This means the resurrection victory of Jesus is a living reality for us. It transforms everything that we do, because we know that God is with us, and that he has defeated the powers of evil once and for all in Jesus Christ. St. Paul says in Romans 8:35 and 37: 'Who shall separate us from the love of Christ? Shall tribulation, or distress, or persecution, or famine, or nakedness, or peril, or sword? . . . No, in all these things we are more than conquerors through him who loved us.'

Our God reigns. In March, 1990 Cecil and Myrtle Kerr from the Rostrevor Community in Northern Ireland visited our church. The Rostrevor Community has for many years been involved in the ministry of reconciliation in the suffering and deeply divided society of Northern Ireland.

Cecil Kerr spoke to us of our need to look to our Lord who reigns. In all the problems that we face, we must not allow the evil one to have the last word. 'Christians should come together,' he said, 'and together proclaim, especially in situations of violence, that Jesus is Lord.' This means that we must go to one another and be with one another, where there is violence and suffering. The lessons which have been learnt by Christians in Northern Ireland speak very powerfully and relevantly to us in South Africa.

It is the knowledge of the Lordship and victory of Jesus that gives us hope. But more than this, our hope flows from seeing God at work as we step out in faith and obedience. Those who are doing something positive in faith are those who have hope for the future; those who are paralysed by fear and a sense of helplessness are those who are most prey to despair.

Cecil and Myrtle Kerr reminded us of some principles which we ourselves had been learning in our own situation in Natal. They said, 'In a divided country, reconciliation has to happen by meeting; it has to happen person to person, and there have to be meeting places; and these have to be peopled by those who have a heart for the unity which God wants.' The world needs to see a demonstration of reconciliation in Christ, not simply to hear more words. 'If you have relationships across the community then when a tragedy or crisis comes, you have the basis for doing something for God's glory.' That has been exactly our experience in Hilton and Sweetwaters.

On the Sunday evening of their visit, Cecil Kerr preached in our church. He said that in looking for solutions for South Africa, we must not take our eyes off Jesus. We must proclaim the Lordship of Jesus wherever we can, and we must do it across the barriers. He pointed us to Ephesians 2:13–14. 'But now in Christ Jesus you who once were far off have been brought near in the blood of Christ. For he is our peace, who has made us both one, and has broken down the dividing wall of hostility.'

Cecil Kerr spoke to us from his own experience in Ireland of the urgency of finding unity amongst God's people as we face the forces of evil. In all our weakness, we are the light of the world, and this is an enormous reponsibility. 'Every time we meet together across the divide, God honours it,' he said, 'and especially when we bear witness to Jesus across the divide.'

These words are very relevant for the church in South Africa. We have so many opportunities to break down the barriers that divide us, the barriers of race, culture, economic status and many others. But this can only be done in Christ, because he is the one who is our peace, who died and rose again, in order to 'reconcile us both to God in one body through the cross, thereby bringing the hostility to an end'. (Eph. 2:16) This is where the hope for South Africa, and for the world, truly lies. Our hope lies in the cross and resurrection of Jesus. The message of reconciliation has been entrusted to the church of the Lord Jesus Christ. We have been given the responsibility of proclaiming, in word and deed, the Good News of peace, peace with God, and peace among all people.

All this is from God, who through Christ

reconciled us to himself and gave us the ministry of reconciliation; that is, in Christ God was reconciling the world to himself ... So we are ambassadors for Christ, God making his appeal through us. We beseech you on behalf of Christ, be reconciled to God. (2 Cor. 5:18, 19a, 20)

This is the hope of the world: Jesus Christ, the one who was born Prince of Peace: 'And suddenly there was with the angel a multitude of the heavenly host praising God and saying, "Glory to God in the highest, and on earth peace among men with whom he is pleased!"' (Luke 2:13–14)

Over the past years, this prayer has been used many times by Christians in Pietermaritzburg:

A prayer for peace in Pietermaritzburg.

Lord Jesus Christ, whose birth signified peace on earth, we lift to you the suffering people of our city ravaged by violence.

You call peacemakers blessed; we pray for the anointing by your Spirit of those working for peace.

Lord Jesus Christ, Prince of Peace we pray that you will dispel all fear, hate and the quest for power, and bring peace to our city and our land. Amen.

Becoming a people of hope

When we know personally and corporately the power of the death and resurrection of Jesus,

The Way Forward – Our God Reigns

we become a people of hope. Hope flows from our knowledge of the power and the victory of Jesus Christ. Our hope cannot be based upon political or economic plans or expectations. These may sometimes bring about an improvement in people's living conditions, but they cannot change people's hearts. Only the message of the gospel can bring about the change that is really needed in this land. In South Africa today many people have little hope for the future of the nation. Politically, things often seem very dark and depressing.

It is particularly in times such as these that the church must be a people of hope and optimism and courage. Our hope and optimism do not spring from political ideals and expectations. It springs from our knowledge of the love of God in Jesus Christ his Son, and of his love for every person living on this earth. As God's people we must also be people-centred. Our God is above all concerned about people, not about ideologies, or doctrines or traditions. We have a people-centred God. When we become a people-centred church, a church that truly shows the love of Jesus for all people, then we will find within us joy and faith and hope. Love, joy, faith and hope are all inextricably linked in the Christian life. Jesus said: 'This is my commandment, that you love one another as I have loved you.' 'These things I have spoken to you, that my joy may be in you, and that your joy may be full.' (John 15:12, 11)

'So faith, hope, love abide, these three; but the greatest of these is love.' (1 Cor. 13:13)

In South Africa, there cannot be hope for the future unless there is also healing of the past. South Africa is a nation of suffering. Overwhelmingly that suffering has been borne by the black people. Very few white South Africans have experienced the full force of the policy of apartheid and its consequences. The suffering of the people in our parish over the past few years has been minimal when compared to the suffering of those directly caught up in the violence. Yet because we cannot simply remain detached and aloof from what is going on around us, we also have been traumatized. It is hard to live in such a society. It is especially hard when one knows that many of those who are suffering in places like Sweetwaters are our brothers and sisters in Christ. There is a real sense in which, by becoming identified with those who are suffering, we also have been a suffering community. Thus we have needed healing and restoration. I am sure that many, many South Africans, black and white, carry very deep scars as a result of what has happened in our nation, especially over the past ten years or so. We need, many of us, to find a place and a time where we can be touched deep within by the healing Spirit of God. This is the inward journey, the journey to wholeness which leads through the valleys of pain and testing, and brings us to a greater and greater identification with Jesus Christ himself. As we become more like him through sharing in his sufferings and his victory, so we become, more and more, whole people, because we are drawing closer and closer to the heart of God. As we experience the reality of God's love in the midst of our pain we are set free from many deep-rooted insecurities and burdens. We are set free by the love of God, to be people who are able to reach out in that love to a suffering world.

The Way Forward – Our God Reigns

South Africans of all colours need this healing, because the divisions in our society run very deep. Sometimes our attitudes and responses to one another have been conditioned and ingrained over many years, even generations. Crossing the divides in our society is risky and difficult. For many white people, it is not that they don't know that this is necessary and important, but rather that they feel impotent, even paralysed, through fear, or guilt, or simply because all the points of reference from their past are unable to help them to face these new and testing challenges. Yet healing and reconciliation will not happen unless we are prepared to act, and to take risks. The Lord's call is for us to go his way in obedience and faith. This alone is the way to the healing and wholeness that we need, but this is not an easy route for many of us to take.

It is not easy for us to go and serve the poor, yet when we are willing to do this, we find that we are the ones who gain, because the poor have so much to give us. We can learn so much from them, and through them we receive the gift of hope. Sarah Dottridge spoke to me of the way in which her involvement in Sweetwaters has given her hope for the future. She said,

> I am far more hopeful about the future of South Africa than most of my friends, because I know black people. The benefit of this work is a gift that God gives us. It is a gift of hope for the future of the country. People think that we are stupid to go to Sweetwaters because of the risk. There is some risk, but

when you think of the risk that Jesus took in coming down to earth . . .

It is hard for many white South African Christians to go and serve the poor. It is hard for us to let go of our ideas of how things should be done, and the kind of conditions and ways of doing things that we are used to. In order to be able to serve the poor we have to learn the humility of Jesus himself, that self-emptying, that laying-down of our lives, which he has taught us by his own example. And so we discover that it is from the poor that we can learn the humility of Jesus himself.

It is hard to go to the poor. It is costly, and it can even be dangerous. But we always come back enriched. We see their openness to God. The poor know their need of God, and so in them there is usually an immediate acknowledgement of need and a willingness to turn to God for help. If we ask in our white congregation that those who need prayer and ministry remain behind after a service of worship, perhaps two or three will stay. In a black congregation, it is likely to be virtually the whole congregation that will be wanting prayer.

Through our relationships with people in Sweetwaters we receive great joy and encouragement. We see God at work, and hear wonderful expressions of faith and thanksgiving. Recently one of the women from our church, who leads a Bible study group on Tuesday mornings in Sweetwaters, asked the group, 'What have you learnt from coming to the group?' A Zulu woman who has a small child with a badly deformed head stood up. Because she has a crippled child, she had felt that everyone looked at her critically, since the time of the birth of this child. She had been coming regularly to this group for about a year. 'Now that I know that Jesus loves me,' she said, 'I can hold my head up high among my neighbours.'

The love of Jesus shared amongst those who are poor brings joy and hope to our lives, because in this way Christ's love becomes real and powerful to us. It is not cloaked and qualified, as so often happens among those who are preoccupied with the cares and riches of this world. It seems to me that we find God amongst the poor in a way that we find him nowhere else.

When we have been to the poor we know that we have actually been with Jesus. Anthea Garman, writing in the *African Enterprise Update* in November 1988 said,

> A part of AE that deserves special mention is the Bonginkosi team. Some of the most spiritually enlightening times I have spent have been with them, going into the forgotten areas where people are hungry, naked, homeless. It is a small ministry, most often never heard of, but it is powerful in its transformation of people in desperately needy communities.

We know that it is often God's way to work through the weak and hidden things of this world.

It is important to see that hope comes through building personal relationships, especially those which build bridges from one community to another. If we are to work for a better world for our children we must start on the person to person level. Economic and political theories and ideologies will not in themselves bring about a better future.

In this we can learn from the experience of those in other countries who have lived out their lives under totalitarian governments, with very little hope of any major political change. In an interview, published in 1988, Mikhail Epshtein, a Moscow literary critic, spoke about a new kind of optimism which he could see emerging at that time in the Soviet Union.[1] He said,

> The old optimism was that of the pioneers, who believed that they were building a shining future for the whole of mankind. When we came up against the facts – that if we were building a future, it was dark, not shining, we at first experienced a terrible despair: that was the predominant feeling in the 1970s. But we no longer think now in those purely social terms, and the result is that we feel liberated.

The interviewer then commented, 'In the West, I think that a similar disillusionment has resulted in a sense of loss, not liberation.' Epshtein replied,

> Well, perhaps the West still puts too much hope in social change. Your experience has been somewhat different from ours. We've experienced the most powerful attempt at creating a social utopia, and understood its limits. The point is that one needn't be pessimistic about people as such: on the contrary,

> our experience has simply shown that people can't be judged or measured in this way; there's a contradiction between our social conditions and what we really are. We see a separation between 'society' and ourselves, and consider that everything that relates only to 'society' is a dead end. It's not that Utopia has been postponed for somewhere in the future; on the contrary, we've already experienced everything that could be constructed in the name of this utopia – that historical idea has been realized already to the extent that it could be.

He goes on to say,

> What's irresponsible is to take on responsibility for the whole state, society, the world, the lives of millions of anonymous people. That's been our worst crime, and we have started to realize it now. We should moderate our boundaries: look at what's close, not what's far away. I mean this literally. We were told to love distant peoples – to help the blacks in Africa – while all the while we were busy destroying each other at home.

Our hope cannot be based upon large-scale national or international political solutions to our problems. Hope comes from seeing those who are close at hand – our neighbours – and building relationships with them. In particular hope comes through building relationships with the poor and the suffering and allowing the love of Christ to enter in and to fill our lives and our world.

Jesus is leading us to those around us, especially to those who are lost, hurting, sick or poor. In caring for the poor and oppressed we will also be called into conflict with the powers and structures which perpetuate their suffering and poverty. But the primary concern for the church must be to bring the power of the kingdom of God to people, especially to those who are close at hand. Placing our hope in an ideological or political solution to the problems of our society is simply chasing the wind. The only real solution lies in changing the hearts and lives of people, and this is what Jesus Christ does by his power at work in us.

In 2 Corinthians 4:5 Paul writes, 'For what we preach is not ourselves, but Jesus Christ as Lord, with ourselves as your servants for Jesus' sake.' For Paul, serving the Lord Jesus meant becoming a slave, a slave of Christ, and a slave of Christ's people. This, I believe, is where the great challenge lies for Christians in our own day and age. For Paul and the New Testament, serving the Lord Jesus Christ was a total all-encompassing commitment of one's whole life. I believe that God is calling those who in these days will give themselves wholly to him and his purposes. He is calling us to costly obedience and faith, to live and work for the proclamation in power of the Lordship of Jesus Christ to the modern world, in word and deed.

NOTES

Chapter Three

1 From The Servant Song by Richard Gillard, in Cry Hosanna, edited by Betty Pulkingham and Mimi Farra, (Hodder and Stoughton, London, 1980).

Chapter Six

1 See Michael Cassidy, *The Passing Summer*, (London, Hodder & Stoughton, 1989), p 346.

Chapter Eight

1 Quoted in *Clarion Call*, Vol 2, 1988, p 21.
2 Quoted in *Clarion Call*, Vol 2, 1988, p 21.
3 *Sunday Tribune*, October 14, 1990, p 16.
4 *The Natal Witness*, May 9, 1990.

Chapter Nine

1 'PACSA Newsletter', August, 1990, No 44.
2 *Echo*, Thursday, May 10, 1990.
3 *The Natal Witness*, June 15, 1990.

Chapter Ten

1 See also Matthew 25:31–46; Amos 5:10–15; Psalm 94; Isaiah 3:13–15; and 1 John 3:17–18.

Chapter Thirteen

1. Malcolm Muggeridge, *Something Beautiful for God*, (London, Collins, 1971), p 118.
2. Gerard Hughes, *God of Surprises*, (London, DLT, 1985), p 22.
3. Michael Wooderson, *Good News Down the Street*, (Grove Books, Nottingham).
4. *Sunday Tribune*, March 31, 1991, p 18.
5. *Sunday Tribune*, March 31, 1991, p 18.

Chapter Fourteen

1. Quoted in *Seek*, September 1988, p 11.
2. Quoted in *Seek*, September 1988, p 11.
3. Malcolm Muggeridge, *Something Beautiful for God*, (London, Collins, 1971), p 68. See also Chapter 6 on the 'Discipline of Simplicity' in *The Celebration of Discipline* by Richard Foster, (London, Hodder & Stoughton, 1980).

Chapter Fifteen

1. Gerard Hughes, *God of Surprises*, (London, DLT, 1985), p 70.

Chapter Sixteen

1. Index of Censorship 1/88.